THE UNTO
PETER FLEMING A

UNFOLDING
DESTINIES

OLIVE FLEMING LIEFELD

edited by Verne Becker

ZondervanPublishingHouse
Grand Rapids, Michigan

A Division of HarperCollins*Publishers*

UNFOLDING DESTINIES
The Untold Story of Peter Fleming and the Auca Mission
Copyright © 1990 by Olive Fleming Liefeld

Requests for information should be addressed to:
Zondervan Publishing House
1415 Lake Drive S.E.
Grand Rapids, Michigan 49506

Library of Congress Cataloging-in-Publication Data

Liefeld, Olive Fleming.
    Unfolding destinies : the untold story of Peter Fleming and the
Auca mission / Olive Fleming Liefeld.
        p. cm.
    ISBN 0-310-54001-1
    1. Fleming, Peter, d. 1956. 2. Huao Indians—Missions. 3. Huao
Indians—Social conditions. 4. Missionaries—Ecuador—Biography.
5. Church of the Brethren—Missions—Ecuador—Title.
F3722.1H83F545 1990
266'.0092—dc20
[B]   90–46134
                                                                CIP

The excerpts from *The Journals of Jim Elliot* have been used with the kind
permission of Fleming H. Revell, publishers, Old Tappan, N.J. Copyright ©
by Fleming H. Revell, 1983.

Printed in the United States of America

90 91 92 93 94 / AK / 10 9 8 7 6 5 4 3 2 1

Contents

Acknowledgments

I want to thank all those who over the years have encouraged me to write Pete's story. From the beginning Elisabeth Elliot urged me to write about Pete. In recent years it was through Ruth Tucker's interest in Pete's role and her probing of my thoughts that I began to write. Stan Gundry of Zondervan and his wife, Pat, both encouraged me to proceed with the project. Pete's brother, Ken Fleming, had in mind editing Pete's diary but agreed to my doing the story instead. I am grateful to my friend Linda Cannell for the hours she spent going over the original draft, giving me valuable "first impressions" and making editorial suggestions. I would be without the final chapter if not for Rachel Saint. She made it possible for me to meet with various groups of Waorani people for the first time. I cannot thank her enough for that privilege and for her hospitality to Walt, Holly, and me at her jungle home. Kimo and Dawa, our constant companions in the jungles, shared their still-vivid memories of the killing. Verne Becker did the final editing. I appreciate the hours he spent going over the material, asking me searching questions to enhance the narrative, and yet allowing me to tell my own story. This story would not have been possible except for the constant love and encouragement of my husband, Walt, as I began to relive those days with my first husband. Our three children, David, Beverly, and Holly, have also been my loving supporters.

Foreword

*"U*nfolding Destinies!" As I think of these words I am aware that my own destiny is one of those affected by the death of Pete Fleming and four other missionaries who attempted to bring God's love to Ecuadorian Indians known then as Aucas—"savages." As Olive's "new" husband—that's how I was introduced to the Aucas after thirty-one years of marriage—I am conscious that my life has been deeply affected not only maritally but spiritually. And you who are reading this now are about to be affected also.

The "unfolding" has taken place over many decades, before and after as well as during the attempt to reach the Aucas. They, by the way, are now known by their real tribal name, Waorani. Some of this unfolding has taken place in our own family during Olive's writing of the manuscript and during our visit to the Waorani in January 1989.

Many friends have asked me how it has affected Olive to live through her early experiences once again. Naturally most people think mainly of her bereavement. But as the story will show, there were other times, less traumatic, of course, but in their own way painful, when recollection brought tears. My own deepest emotions came on the beach by the Curaray River where the men were killed. You will read how these recollections and some new revelations of Kimo and Dawa, one of the killers and his wife, brought a new perspective to it all.

You will understand why I am still moved at the very memory of that scene.

Some have asked how it has affected me and our children to have Olive write about her first husband. I have always lived in awe of Pete. It was not easy being married to the widow of such a devoted missionary and martyr. Even more I have been deeply conscious of being married to one whom God trusted to suffer and participate in an experience of such magnitude and Christian significance. If that consciousness ever faded during the years of our marriage it certainly has been strongly and even painfully revived by the many months of remembrance and writing.

The experience of reading about her first love has been eased by her sincere and delicate narration. The love and respect our children and I have for her has been deepened in the process. It is not trite to say we went through this together. Perhaps you will gain some insight into this when I tell you about Olive's rings. When I bought her engagement ring I unknowingly selected one almost identical to the one Pete had given her. Several years ago we had a jeweler friend design a new ring. It has two diamonds—Pete's and mine.

It would have been superficial for Olive to skim over early love and experiences and come quickly to the Auca experience. It also would have been a distortion of the true humanness of Pete, Jim, and their companions simply to celebrate their faith and strength. That would hardly give credit to their God who developed that faith and strength in very human people. I watched Olive as she struggled to portray this humanness while avoiding the character demolition so common in literature. Sometimes we even discussed the adverbs and adjectives that would best bring balance.

Olive's deepest concern, however, and mine as well, has always been to understand why the men died. That includes the reason the Aucas decided to kill them, the question of whether the missionaries were in some way responsible—some have charged there was inadequate preparation—and, most intense of all, the reason God allowed it. Others have pondered this and some, like Elisabeth Elliot (whom you will meet in this book as Betty Howard), have written thoughtfully about God's "will."

During the course of our life together Olive and I have often struggled with the question of why it happened that five young men—strong and gifted, each needed in another part of the missionary endeavor, each married, each (except Pete) a father—were allowed to die. Olive clung to the belief that God had prepared her for it, but had he prepared the events themselves? Was it all evil and the work of demons or Devil? Was it an unfortunate tragedy? Did God do it deliberately?

Many have attempted to justify what happened by the results. Do the scores or hundreds of people who were inspired to consider becoming missionaries justify it? Do the hundreds of Aucas who became Christians explain its purpose? Does the abandonment of mutual killing among the Aucas (except for a remote group still in darkness) warrant the loss? How about the fact that all of the killers became believers and that three of them are now pastors and evangelists? Does any of this say to us, "*This* is why it happened"? If so, then the next question is: Was the infinitely wise and powerful God unable to find a way other than to sacrifice the lives of such men as these, and five of them at that? All such talk about this subject is, of course, hindsight.

Bring in the theologians and the philosophers. Let them sit with grieving widows and philosophize about whether God causes, contributes, allows, redirects, or whatever. Is God's will cold or loving? Is his will impersonal fate or personal care? Hidden or understandable? To be feared or good?

Grief-stricken people are often "comforted" with a Bible verse popularly known by its reference, Romans 8:28: "And we know that in all things God works for the good of those who love him, who have been called according to his purpose" (NIV). I put "comforted" in quotes because sometimes the verse is quoted mechanically or unfeelingly and sometimes as a substitute for personal deeds of comfort. Some think a grieving person only needs to apprehend a theological truth. The message some think that verse conveys is that we should welcome evil or that evil always comes from God and is intended to accomplish some hidden purpose.

The verse, of course, does not say that. Nor does it say, on the contrary, that all things are good. It does not say that everything is directly caused by God. The Bible, in fact, calls death an "enemy" (1 Corinthians 15:26) and says that Christ died to destroy the Devil, "who holds the power of death" (Hebrews 2:14). What Romans 8:28 does communicate is the truth that God can take all things—even bad ones—and bring good from them for those who love him. It teaches that God acts purposefully in calling us to faith in him. It reflects a loving God.

Our decades-long quest to understand Romans 8:28 better as it applies to the events on the Curaray River received unforeseen assistance through an invitation to a conference in neighboring Colombia, which opened the way to visit Ecuador. That trip brought a further "unfolding" of destinies. But I leave the next phase to Olive's story.

Walter L. Liefeld

1
THE STORY

On Thursday, January 12, 1956, I stood in the bedroom of the Saints' house in Shell Mera, Ecuador, my arms crossed, my eyes fixed on Air Force Major Nurnberg and Navy Captain DeWitt. Also in the room were four other missionary wives: Marjorie Saint, Elisabeth (Betty) Elliot, Marilou McCully, and Barbara Youderian. We were trying to take in what the major had just told us—that the bodies of our husbands, who had been missing after they made face-to-face contact with the savage Auca Indians, had been found floating in the Curaray River. No one had as yet been positively identified, since the bodies had been spotted by helicopter, but as he read one of the descriptions from his notebook, my heart sank.

"This one had on a red belt of some woven material," he said.

Immediately the other four women looked at me. We all knew.

"That was Pete," I said numbly.

The watches and rings the search party brought us a few days later ended our anxious wait. There was no question—Pete, Nate, Jim, Ed, and Roger were dead.

During the search, we desperately hoped that at least one of the men had gotten away. Each sighting of a white man, or a fire deep in the jungle, momentarily raised our hopes. But in my heart I knew they were dead even before the captain and the major had arrived. At least I didn't have to wait any longer.

Even so, when the final word came, the sense of loss overwhelmed me. I knew the truth, but couldn't accept the reality of what had happened to my husband, Pete. Whether I felt God's presence at that point I cannot recall; I do remember the assurance from his Word, however. During the week of waiting and hoping I read 2 Corinthians 5:5: "He who has prepared us for this very thing is God." Somehow God was explaining the turmoil Pete and I had experienced for the last four-and-a-half years. He had not only prepared Pete for this day; he had also prepared me. Nevertheless, my emotions swung from one extreme to another in the days that followed: grief over my loss, trust in God's sovereignty, anger at the men for taking a foolish risk, confidence in God's Word, and fear that he was punishing me for my lack of faith. My dreams turned to nightmares.

I left Ecuador for good in March of 1957, bringing to a close the chapter of my life as a foreign missionary. At that time I struggled not only with my still-fresh grief, but also with a real sense of defeat. The other four widows stayed on in Ecuador; Betty and Barbara went back to the jungles, while Marj and Marilou carried on a ministry in Quito. Betty was already praying that she might be used to reach the Aucas.

Since missionaries rarely left the field in those days, many people at home questioned my decision. Some even quoted the verse, "No one who puts his hand to the plow and looks back is fit for the kingdom of God" (Luke 9:62). All I could do was trust my sense of God's leading and listen to the advice I received from godly friends. The God who had prepared me for my short time with Pete would also guide me in the next step. Though I wanted some answers right away, it was not to be. My source of comfort was from Scripture: "Be still, and know that I am God" (Psalm 46:10). "In quietness and in trust shall be your strength" (Isaiah 30:15). No great revelation, but simply the assurance that God was who he was and that I could trust him.

Along with grief and defeat came the reality of being a widow at twenty-three. What would I do? How would I support myself? Returning home didn't help: I had no career credentials, since I hadn't completed my major at the University of Washington. I had training in missionary medicine, but only for jungle work. For all of Pete's initial concern not to go to the Aucas married because of the danger involved, once we were married we never talked about what I'd do if he were killed.

Having no children only intensified my loneliness. I found it hard to be with my married friends. Their joy with each other and with their children only made me more conscious of my loss. It was hard to pick up where I had left off three years before. The kind, well-meaning words of people telling me it was all for the best and that God knew what he was doing brought me little comfort.

Some weeks after the men had been killed, Betty and I had talked about remarriage and what the Bible said about it. Because we were all young we knew it was a possibility. But I wasn't ready to think about remarriage yet—the grief was too new. Later, as people tried to reassure me, they would often say that God had someone else for me. I found this hard to accept: I was still a newlywed, married for barely eighteen months. Pete was the only man for me. How could I think of there being someone else? Moreover, the media publicity in *Life* magazine and national newspapers made me vulnerable to all kinds of strange proposals and requests. I received some letters from men (with photos!) who were fully persuaded that God had especially prepared me for them. One man wrote that he was so convinced that it was God's will for him to marry me that he knew I'd accept even though we'd never met.

While I struggled with the realities of widowhood and media attention, letters came in, reporting that hundreds of young people in Christian colleges had dedicated their lives to missions. I was told that my husband had not died in vain. I tried to praise God for working in the lives of these people. I told myself that this was what we had hoped for. But inside I wondered whether "results" such as these rendered Pete's death any less meaningless. I began to question our human concept of God's will. We all wanted to make sense out of this loss, yet without attributing any mistake to God. It was his will, we all said. Therefore if God had led Jim and Pete and the others each step of the way, it meant that *all* was done according to his will, without mistake. Something about this logic bothered me. I couldn't accept the final conclusion that their death was God's will. If it was, then God's actions, if indeed they were his, seemed harsh and hollow.

Though most people responded compassionately to the tragedy, many did not. Some said it was a terrible waste. But I wondered if these people thought it a waste to risk one's life in other adventures, such as climbing Mt. Everest. Others felt it served the men right for intruding where they weren't wanted. "Leave those people alone," they'd say. "Don't destroy their culture." Even some missionaries grumbled that so much attention had been focused on the Aucas and the five widows that their own ministry had suffered neglect by supporters at home. As the good and the bad responses weighed in, God seemed to be hanging in the balance. Did we need to vindicate God's actions with results? What if the Aucas were never converted? Would the death of five men be justified?

Meanwhile, the huge numbers of young people supposedly "called" into missions seemed to fade away. Commitments were forgotten. Contrary to what we had heard, armies of young missionaries were not going into the jungles of Ecuador to replace the five men. I was left with my questions. Why would God take five seasoned missionaries from the work he had prepared them for? His will seemed unreasonable, uncaring. But how could I possibly know God's mind and his purposes anyway?

Back in Ecuador, some of the missionaries who remained had made a second attempt to establish an air-to-ground friendship with the Aucas through gift drops. Then, at the end of 1957, a major breakthrough occurred: Two Auca women appeared at a Quichua settlement. Only a year later, Betty Elliot, her little daughter, Valerie, and Rachel Saint (Nate's sister) were actually living with the Aucas—an answer to many prayers. (For an inside view of this period in Auca history, read *The Dayuma Story,* by Ethel Emily Wallis and *The Savage, My Kinsman,* by Elisabeth Elliot.) It appeared that God's plan for the Aucas was beginning to unfold. The world took another look at the Aucas as *Life* magazine visited the Auca village to follow up on the story, telling it this time through Betty's eyes.

During the next few years, Betty faithfully wrote the other four widows with any information she could get from the Aucas. We all wanted to know just what had gone on in their minds when they encountered our husbands. Why had the Indians been so friendly at first—as the men had reported over the radio—only to rise up suddenly and kill them? As Betty learned more of the Auca language, she managed to put together some of the pieces of what had happened. She discovered that the Aucas had mistakenly concluded the men were cannibals, and had killed them out of fear.

As a new era began for the Aucas, my life also moved in a new direction. In 1958 I traveled to Schroon Lake, New York, for a summer of counseling at the Word of Life camp, then stayed that fall to work as secretary to the president of Shelton College, a small Christian school in northern New Jersey. At

homecoming weekend I met a man by the name of Walter
Liefeld, who was president of the school's alumni association. I
had never heard of him, but he said he knew about me. (I later
learned that he had prayed for an opportunity to meet me.)
That fall I kept hearing his name in connection with various
New York ministries. He had served as an Inter-Varsity
Christian Fellowship staff member and continued to speak for
IVCF as well as in area churches and conferences. He was
currently studying for his Ph.D. at Columbia University.
Something about him interested me. At one point he wrote me
a brief letter with some information I had wanted. He added a
P.S. that said, "This does not need to be answered." Because of
the weird proposals I had recently received from some men, I
decided to be cautious and not answer his letter. I didn't expect
to see him again.

Happily, I was mistaken. Our paths crossed again the last
week of December. Our courtship was straightforward and
uncomplicated. It did not take long before I knew that Walt
loved me, by the way he looked at me, by his kindness to me,
and by his frequent calls. His words of love were open,
persuasive, and unqualified. I felt I had lived a lifetime already
and knew what was important to me. Walt and I had a
common sense of direction and purpose. After Pete was killed, I
had wondered whether I could ever love anyone again. Now I
realized I could. By February we both knew that God had
brought us together.

In March 1959, Sam Saint, Nate's oldest brother, announced our engagement at a Word of Life council meeting; in
June we were married in a small, quiet wedding ceremony. We
had received three offers of free honeymoon accommodations
and gladly accepted two: Florida and the Bahamas. Many
Christians in the Bahamas knew about me because they had
followed reports about the death of the five men on HCJB radio
from Ecuador. To them I was still Olive Fleming, while Walt

was an unknown. They warmly welcomed us both, but I naturally got the most attention. We even made the front page of the Nassau newspaper with the headline, EVANGELISTS HONEYMOONING.

For the first five years of our marriage, Walt had a ministry at Sea Cliff Chapel in Long Island, New York, where our son, David, and daughter, Beverly, were born. We moved to Deerfield, Illinois, when Walt accepted a teaching position in New Testament at Trinity Evangelical Divinity School. Our third child, Holly, came along a few years later. Although one of Walt's early dreams had been to teach overseas, he found great fulfillment in training many young men and women who later went into Christian ministries overseas and at home. He also taught many international students, who then returned to their countries as evangelists, pastors, and Bible teachers.

As Walt's ministry grew, I got involved in his teaching and with student wives. Our rich life and ministry together and the gift of three wonderful children filled my heart with thanksgiving to God. I compared myself to Job, who after all his troubles received from God "twice as much as he had before" (Job 42:10). My reputation as the widow of Peter Fleming faded into the background. Although my past seemed more like a series of dreams—some joyful, some tragic—I never forgot it.

I tried to keep up with the Auca situation as the years passed. Through the pioneering efforts of Betty Elliot, Rachel Saint, and others, many of these once-savage people had put down their lances and converted to Christianity. Occasionally something about them popped up in the news media. In 1968 Rachel brought two Auca tribesmen with her to the United States, and I had the awesome privilege of a face-to-face meeting with Kimo, one of the actual men who had killed Pete. He was now a Christian. By the mid-1970s I had lost touch with developments among the Aucas except for hearing a rare

15

news item. But I continued to pray for them, and I hoped that one day I might return to visit them, these people who had changed the course of my life.

*   *   *

That day finally came on January 12, 1989, exactly thirty-three years after I learned of Pete's death. With Walt and our twenty-year-old daughter, Holly, I stood for the first time on what was left of "Palm Beach," the actual spot on the Curaray River where the men had been killed. Kimo and his wife, Dawa, and Rachel Saint served as our guides.

Over the years I have been encouraged to write Pete's story. I not only questioned the value of such a story after so many years, but I also knew his story was my story, with all my memories. I wrestled with the fact that I would be exposing the feelings of my first marriage and the doubts and questions that came with widowhood. Was I willing for that kind of exposure, and was it really fair to Walt and our children? We all saw the value, and so they encouraged me to write it. Walt not only gave his full blessing to the project, but has provided invaluable help and support as well.

Besides unleashing a flood of memories, the trip back to Ecuador proved far more illuminating than I ever would have imagined. I not only gained a whole new appreciation for Pete's efforts to reach the Aucas, but I also learned previously unknown information about the events surrounding his death. These new details add a dramatic, supernatural dimension to the story. I came home with the ending for my manuscript and a reason for telling Pete's story.

What follows is my account of Pete Fleming's life with me, Jim Elliot, our families, and our friends as we struggled together to understand and do God's will, even in the face of death. I also describe my return, with Walt and Holly, to the site where the five men were killed, and the startling yet wonderful things we learned there. Though preparing this book has helped me to put many of my own questions to rest, I believe it serves a greater purpose and speaks to a wider audience. Yes, it will interest those who have followed the still-unfolding plot of one of the most gripping missionary stories of this century. But most important, I believe it will give insight to those who are trying to understand (or help others understand) God's call to ministry.

By telling Pete's story, I hope to show that in spite of his and Jim's idealism and single-minded devotion to God, the choices they made in the course of their ministry were seldom clear-cut. They strove to learn and do God's will, but often did not know exactly what his will was. At various times they wrestled with feelings of doubt, discouragement, and failure. They made mistakes. They didn't always agree on things. They sometimes followed the advice of others, and sometimes ignored it.

I share their human struggles not to satisfy perverse curiosity or to minimize their spiritual stature. On the contrary, I believe their faith and determination will stand out all the more clearly. They had the same questions we all have about the call of God and its implications. They had to deal with human passions as well as spiritual passion, romantic love as well as Christian love, pain as well as joy. In short, Pete Fleming's life parallels that of all who trust God and honestly seek his direction for their life. Giving one's whole self to God is never easy; the way is seldom clear. But perhaps by looking more closely at Pete's life, and his relationship with me, Jim Elliot, and the other missionaries, some light may be shed on the mysterious process of ascertaining the will, and the call, of God.

2
PETE,
THE "BRAIN"

*T*he youngest of three children—perhaps indicated by his initials, P.S.—Peter Sillence Fleming sat in front of me Sunday after Sunday in the Brethren "assembly" we attended in Seattle.* I saw every unrestrained wiggle. Although we knew each other early in life, Pete was three years older, and the age difference limited our friendship at first. He usually ran off with his friends after the service, while I stayed by my parents. My strongest early memories, therefore, are less of Pete and more of his fun-loving father, Kenneth, who teased me unmercifully. Pete's mother, Greta, on the other hand, had a sweet, quiet disposition. She shared her love of books with her children; Kenneth, his love for the English language. At dinner, Dad led the family in vocabulary-building exercises. He wanted his children to know the meaning and the proper use of words. As a result, they gained an impressive command of the language. (Pete would later become an impossible opponent in Scrabble. Not until he encountered Betty Howard in Ecuador would he meet his match.)

---

*The Brethren are a small but vital fellowship of Christians; they call their churches *assemblies*.

Another gift Pete received from his parents was a deep love for music. He took great pleasure in singing the old hymns of the faith and in listening to classical music. Every other Saturday night for years, the Flemings opened their home to the young people of the assembly for "singing practice." All singles (high school and older) were welcome, regardless of singing ability. Kenneth Fleming somehow took those untrained voices and produced a fine group of singers for the Sunday evening gospel service. I looked forward to joining the group when I began high school.

The Flemings lived in a large old Victorian on Queen Ann Hill, near the center of Seattle. It had spacious rooms and high ceilings, and was the only house Pete ever lived in before going to the mission field.

As that squirmy little boy in the pew grew into a teenager, his restlessness in church continued. His mother in her wisdom gave Pete and his older brother Ken a choice: Either sit quietly through the worship service, or go home after Sunday school and prepare dinner. I was envious that Pete could leave while I had to sit through what most of us kids considered to be a boring service.

If Pete and I had lived in the age of computer matchmaking, we never would have made it, probably never would have met. Although we grew up in the same church and professed the same personal faith in Christ (he, at age twelve through a blind evangelist, and I at age ten at a Bible camp), our printouts would have shown that we had very little in common.

My background did not allow for the love of literature and music that Pete had. My parents, Olive and Alex Ainslie, had been raised in a very conservative Brethren group in Canada, and read nothing but the Bible and books related to the Bible. I never went to the library as a child, so I only read from the few books available through school. My mother encouraged me to take piano lessons, but I soon realized that my parents neither understood nor appreciated classical music. (The little gospel hall my mother grew up in forbade the use of instruments for the worship of God, and discouraged musical training generally.) I believe my mother wanted me to have the musical opportunity she never had, but she never encouraged me very strongly. Meanwhile, my father wanted me to play only hymns, not Bach or Beethoven or the popular songs I practiced. Their attitude frustrated me, and I didn't like my piano teacher anyway, so I quit taking lessons.

My father was a practical, down-to-earth man who cared about people and above all else tried to show Christ's love to them. As a door-to-door deliveryman for a bakery, he got to know his customers personally and shared his faith with many of them. They came to depend on him not just for bread, but for pastoral care as well. He always made himself available to people in need. When he learned, for instance, that some of his rural customers had no nearby church to attend, he and my mother started several Sunday schools for the children in those areas. My mother also hosted a neighborhood Bible study, and was always willing to open our home to others.

One year on Christmas Eve my father received a late-night phone call from a distraught wife on his delivery route who didn't know where her alcoholic husband was. Immediately my father went out, driving from tavern to tavern, looking for her husband who needed to be with his family for Christmas.

My father also loved the outdoors, and passed on that love to me. He taught me all kinds of sports—ice skating, horseback riding, swimming, and my very favorite sport, skiing. In short, Pete and I both had loving, Christian parents who modeled godly living to us and to the community. The main difference was that Pete had much more access to "secular" knowledge and culture than I.

When Pete was sixteen, his mother died suddenly—a terrible shock to the family and their friends. It was a difficult time in Pete's life, though I didn't know this until years later. According to Pete's classmate Evan Cochrane, Pete's faith at that time had made a strong impression on his friends at Queen Ann High School. Much to their surprise, Pete showed up at school the very day after his mother's death. When asked why he had come, he said, "Humanly I feel very sad and at a loss, but spiritually my God is able to sustain, and I know it is just a matter of time when I will see my mother again in heaven."

During Pete's high school years, one man in particular profoundly influenced his growth as a Christian. His name was Lorne Sanny, who came to Seattle to direct a relatively new Christian organization, The Navigators. Pete joined a Bible study group Lorne had started for Christian high school boys. As they studied the Word together and memorized Scripture, Pete learned the importance of personal Bible study, became more disciplined in his lifestyle, and soon had committed hundreds of verses to memory. His life took on new depth and meaning, and he became more intentional in witnessing to his friends.

Though Pete found it easy to share his Christian faith—largely because of Lorne Sanny's encouragement—his classmates did not view him as fanatical. They respected him and treated him as "one of the boys." No doubt Pete's athletic ability helped him earn this respect. Whatever the sport—basketball, baseball, Ping-Pong, tennis, or golf—he played hard and he played to win. He received a varsity letter for his golf performance, and was soon invited to be the chaplain of the Boys Club, a group of lettermen from various sports that ran the school's social events. At first he hesitated to take the position, concerned that other Christians at school would misunderstand. But because he deeply wanted God to use his life among the other guys, he finally accepted the offer. From then on, Pete opened each meeting of the Boys Club with prayer. One member later recalled how sincere and relevant Pete's prayers were, and that God used them to touch many of those young men for Christ.

At his high school commencement in 1946, Pete spoke on the subject of "Building a Foundation." Memories of World War II and the atomic bomb were very fresh in everyone's minds. In a world ravaged by war, a world seeking permanence amid an uneasy peace, Pete said, a strong foundation was needed, and that foundation could be found in the Bible.

Pete had also gotten involved in Youth for Christ while in high school. Now eighteen and trying to find his way around the huge University of Washington campus, Pete was befriended by YFC's new area director, Willis Shank. To Pete's amazement, Willis always took time to talk with him no matter how busy he was or how small Pete's problem. Willis was also a great entertainer who knew how to bring young people together and give them a good time. One night, Pete sat enthralled as Willis demonstrated his unusual musical ability, hamming it up on the saxophone, tapping tunes on musical water glasses, playing a musical saw, and (Pete's favorite) screeching out songs on a "violin" made from a battered oil can—all to the delight of the young people present.

At one point, Pete asked Willis to sponsor a basketball team he and some of his friends had formed. His response? He had already been praying about starting a YFC basketball team, and would love to help them. "It exceeded even my wildest dreams," Pete later wrote. "Equipment, suits, warm-ups, jackets and big games."

A year later Willis Shank was dead, the victim of a plane crash while on his way to dedicate a mission in Alaska. Pete had lost a close friend and mentor. In his grief he wrote down all the ways Willis had ministered to him and others in that one short year: "His smile and ready wit won him many friends,

and his showmanship and leadership spearheaded his rallies."
Recalling the time Willis had played all the wacky instruments,
Pete wrote,

> It was that night at home that I decided that his life was
> dedicated to the greatest ministry in the world: being a
> friend to friendless young fellas. . . . He was never too
> busy for a friend. I would sit in his office and talk for
> hours, though his desk was always piled with unfinished
> work. But best of all, he not only befriended me but led
> me to the Friend which sticketh closer than a brother.
> And I've often thought since then that American young
> people do not need more youth organizations but more
> friends—friends like Willis Shank. Any young person
> will leave a cold street for a warm heart.

Lorne Sanny and Willis Shank had done far more than
simply teach Pete the Word and give him Bible study tools.
They had poured themselves into his life and served as
significant role models.

Life and learning at a secular university put Pete's faith to
the test. He majored in philosophy, on which few Christians at
that time had articulated a biblical perspective. The intellectual
challenge led him to grapple with and reexamine his Christian
beliefs. As he searched the Scriptures for insight, he found that
he did not need to discard biblical truth; instead, he was able to
establish his faith even more firmly. Realizing his need for
support from other Christian students, he joined the school's
Inter-Varsity Christian Fellowship chapter, eventually serving
as chapter president and teaching a weekly Bible study. In
graduate school, Pete and several of his friends formed a
seminar to study Scripture and theology. They each presented a
paper for the group to read and discuss. The interaction and
close fellowship within this group greatly stimulated Pete's
Christian life and thought.

Pete was in his element on campus. And the more he saw firsthand the need for a strong Christian presence there, the more he began to consider pursuing campus ministry as a teacher of English literature. He had witnessed the influence of one Christian English professor already, and sensed that more like her were needed to actively help Christian young people.

Being three years younger, I was largely unaware of these developments in Pete's life. By the time I entered high school, Pete had already begun at UW. We still attended the same assembly young people's group, however, which included both high-school and college students. My friends and I felt that many of the college students—who far outnumbered us—were dull, snobby, and overly "spiritual." We hesitated to bring our friends to youth group, worried that someone would buttonhole them about "getting saved."

If many of the college students seemed overly "spiritual" to us, Pete qualified as "super-spiritual." He was one of the group's leaders and teachers, and he studied Greek. We all figured he was way above us intellectually. The older ones respected him, but we all thought he was a "brain" who didn't want to have any fun. At one point we were told that Pete was opposed to ice skating; this only reinforced our view of him. At that time, the kids in my age group were wrestling with what it meant to be a committed Christian. We were bristling at the restrictive lifestyle our parents, the church, and the leaders of our youth group imposed on us. Our perception was that fun and spirituality could not go together. We didn't have the foggiest idea of what "spirituality" was; but whatever it was, we didn't want it.

In spite of all this, the young people did manage to have fun together. How could we not, with Seattle and the Pacific Northwest as our playground? To the west lay Puget Sound and its numerous islands; to the east, large lakes perfectly suited to water sports. And if this weren't enough, Mt. Rainier and

Mt. Baker were only a couple of hours away by car. Our group took full advantage of this beautiful country, enjoying water skiing parties and hikes in the summer, and long days of alpine skiing in the winter. I was a passionate skier; Pete, a serious hiker.

All this time I had no interest in a "relationship" with Pete, and was too young for one to develop even if I had wanted it. I seldom saw him at social functions, probably because he was studying. He did bring various girls from the university to church with him, however, and I would assess each one from my vantage point in the row behind him. For a while he dated one girl seriously, it seemed. I decided she would do because she looked like an intellectual, but shortly thereafter they stopped dating and I didn't see her again.

Some time after this "serious" girlfriend departed—on my sixteenth birthday, to be exact—Pete first took notice of me. My parents had spontaneously invited a group of students over for Sunday dinner, as they often did after church. They were all older, and none were close friends of mine, but Pete happened to be among them, along with his brother, Ken, and Ken's girlfriend, Helena. For most of the visit Pete teased me good-naturedly. While we were doing dishes, he kept snapping me with a wet dish towel, trying to get a response from me. Though I loved the attention, I felt shy and said little.

Later that afternoon, someone said that I could knit and had made some socks for my dad—something a girl usually did in those days for her boyfriend. Pete perked up.

"Hey, how about me?" he said, looking my way. "I sure could use some socks. See, mine are full of holes."

He had a pathetic look on his face, and I couldn't tell whether he was still teasing me or not. Before long, the others chimed in, pleading Pete's case, all of which added to my embarrassment. So I ended up agreeing, red-faced, to make him some argyle socks. Pete sat back with a smile, seeming very pleased with himself. I had to admit that I really enjoyed the afternoon. Whenever I saw Pete from then on, he would ask me about my progress on the socks. It gave us something to talk about, and I rather enjoyed the attention.

Some months after the sock episode, our youth group took its annual Memorial Day hike in the Cascade Mountains. While everyone was jockeying for rides in the various cars, I was maneuvered into the back seat of a car with Pete. He acted quite differently than that Sunday in my home. For the entire drive to the mountains, he hardly said a word—not even teasing. All he said was that he had a bad headache. I thought we would never get there. I wondered whether he was upset with me because (he thought) I had manipulated the seating arrangement to be with him. (Even if that had been the case, he certainly had manipulated me to get his pair of socks.) Perhaps he felt concerned that his friends had now seen us together, and he didn't want me to get any ideas. As I sat there trying to figure out what was wrong, I concluded that at sixteen, I was definitely too young for this brainy university fellow.

Pete's behavior that day in the car turned out to be the exception rather than the rule. Most of the time, when we saw each other at youth group functions or church meetings, he did pay some attention to me, though usually in the form of teasing. We dated casually a few times, but I didn't take him seriously, despite the chitchat the group started about "us." My skiing friends kidded me that Pete and I seemed such complete opposites. They couldn't imagine a date with him being any fun. I agreed: He was beyond me intellectually and probably more mature and spiritual as well. After all, I was a junior in high school; he was almost a senior at the university. (He had gone to summer school to graduate in three years.) Another friend told me I wasn't spiritual enough for him, but I knew she only said that because she was interested in Pete herself. Pete probably had to put up with similar cracks from his friends. It was all part of the usual banter within church youth groups.

As I thought about the potential for a relationship with Pete, a new awareness dawned on me: Ultimately, what we did or didn't have in common—sports, music, intellect—wasn't the issue. The real issue, I realized, was that he was totally committed to following the Lord, and somehow I was not. He was developing definite values and opinions about what it meant to be a Christian, and then choosing to live in a certain way as a result. (For instance, I later learned why Pete had given up ice skating—not because he felt it was wrong, but because it had consumed too much of his time and gotten in the way of his commitment to Christ.) I had not yet reached that point in my life; in fact, I had a long way to go. Pete's friends must have picked up on this. Perhaps that's why some of them warned him not to date me. They couldn't imagine a young, immature high-school girl like me fitting into his life. I'm sure I wondered the same thing.

3
GETTING
SERIOUS

Pete got together with me more often during the spring of 1949, my high-school junior year. I was seventeen, and he was now a senior at UW. I say "got together" because I didn't really think of it as dating. We were on such different levels socially and intellectually. I was basically a teeny-bopper with hardly a serious thought in my head. Pete was ultra-intelligent and "super-spiritual" on top of it. That spring we started memorizing the book of Colossians together—a carryover from his Navigator days. I thought of him only as a friend.

During the summer between my junior and senior year, I and a friend agreed to serve as counselors at Camp Imadene, a children's Bible camp on Vancouver Island, just across Puget Sound into Canada. My reason for going? I had nothing better to do, and no other summer jobs were available. I figured I could at least be useful for two months and have fun at the same time. Little did I know that this casual decision would mark a turning point in my life.

My duties at this rustic camp involved counseling, leading cabin devotions, acting as lifeguard, giving swimming lessons, helping with cooking, and working hard wherever I was needed. As I immersed myself in the lives of these children, I realized I was doing things I hadn't done before, and seeing a side of life I hadn't seen before. I had been sheltered from the kind of home life many of the kids were raised in. Many were already hardened against God, even at their young age. Yet as I prayed for and worked with these children, I saw God come alive to some of them, and it profoundly affected me. My eyes were opened to the tremendous spiritual needs of people, even on my own continent. I went home a different person, with a fresh desire to know God.

While at camp, I began to realize that Pete was more interested in me than I thought. He wrote all the time, telling me he missed me. Unsure of my feelings about him, I answered very few of his letters. My experience at camp had awakened me to my need to straighten out my own priorities. At this point, I couldn't even think about being serious with him until I knew where I was going spiritually.

When I arrived home, Pete wondered why I hadn't written very much. He seemed more hurt than disappointed. But he continued to ask me out in the fall, and I noticed my feelings for him were beginning to change. Now it felt more like "dating." It was quite an experience for me, a high school senior, to date an intellectual in graduate school. One could hardly call our dates exciting, especially by today's standards; but no car and no money left us with few options. We finished memorizing the book of Colossians, tackling about ten verses a week, repeating them to each other before our dates. He would whiz through the verses easily, while I struggled each week to have them word perfect. I knew none of my high school friends had dates like mine—and that they wouldn't believe me if I told them what mine were like.

We didn't go to movies; they were taboo among Christians in those days. Shopping malls didn't yet exist. We never even thought of going out to dinner since Pete had no money. We scrimped on hamburgers and hot dogs. Once—and only once—we tried having a tennis date. What a fiasco. Though I was quite coordinated on the ski slopes, swinging a racket somehow didn't suit me. Pete tried to teach me, but I couldn't even return a regular shot, let alone his "killer" serve. A game was out of the question.

Usually our dates involved church activities. Often I would go to a church youth group where he was speaking just to be with him, and that would be our date for the weekend. I didn't mind, however, since we could be together without having to endure the catty comments of young people in our own church.

Once winter arrived, I went skiing whenever I could, usually for the entire day on Saturdays. Often I had to forgo seeing Pete—much to his dismay—in order to ski. At that time, skiing had become a passion for me. Something about whizzing down the powdery slopes exhilarated me, and I had found myself living from ski trip to ski trip. Pete had neither the time nor the money to go, and didn't like missing out on seeing me. Before we got around to dealing with the issue, I wrecked my knee in a nasty ski accident. The doctor told me to hang up my skis for the rest of the year, so Pete and I ended up seeing more of each other after all.

Being barred from the slopes brought about another change in me, however. It forced me to take a hard look at my priorities. I realized that skiing may have taken a similar place in my life that ice skating had taken in Pete's. It wasn't wrong or bad, but it had begun to get in the way of my Christian commitment.

Often Pete and I double dated with one of his friends, David Dye—also an intellectual—and his girlfriend, Bernice. This solved our problem of not having a car, and made it a lot easier for Pete to get me home. (If we couldn't get a ride from someone, I'd have to take an hour-and-a-half bus ride home alone at night—an option I preferred to avoid.) We always sat in the back seat, and Pete would hold my hand.

No matter where we went together, we invariably ended up at Pete's house listening to classical music. Before I ever thought of dating Pete, I enjoyed going to his house on Saturday nights for singing practice. But classical music was another matter: I had no interest in it whatsoever. As Pete and Dave launched into their detailed analysis of movements and themes, I'd yawn. From my limited musical upbringing, I had no foundation to understand classical music, let alone appreciate it. Those two would get so excited about variations on a theme and other such things. "Did you get that?" they'd say to each other at various moments during a piece. "Isn't that wonderful?" I had no idea what they were talking about; it all sounded very complicated and boring to me.

I much preferred the popular music of the day, sung by artists such as Dinah Shore, Perry Como, and Frank Sinatra. My parents objected to it as "worldly," but I still listened to it with my school friends. (I didn't have my own radio or record player.) One of my favorite records was Bing Crosby's "White Christmas." I also liked songs by Irving Berlin and Rodgers and Hammerstein. To me it was so much easier, and far more romantic, to listen to "Some Enchanted Evening" or "People Will Say We're in Love" than some obscure Bach fugue.

Despite my indifference to classical music, I did recognize how much it meant to Pete. For him it was more than an intellectual exercise. Music touched his soul, and he embraced it with great enthusiasm. Besides listening to classical works, he loved to stand around the piano and sing with his father or brother. I realized that if Pete and I were to have a future together, I would have to learn to appreciate his taste in music.

In the spring Pete and I traveled with a carload of my friends to an Easter conference. It was there that I met Jim Elliot's parents for the first time. Mrs. Elliot took one look at me and said, "Aren't you a little young to be going with him?" Pete laughed, but I turned red.

As we rode in the car, my friends took great delight in trying to embarrass me in front of Pete. Above my loud protests, they divulged that I had committed a "secret sin" and never told anyone. When Pete heard what the "sin" was— trying a cigar once—he thought it was hilarious; nevertheless, my friends had succeeded in humiliating me. It was all in fun.

As we got to know each other better, I learned more about what went on in Pete's world, and the issues he wrestled with. He told me of the need he saw for more Christians ministering on secular campuses, and of his resulting desire to pursue a teaching career. I also remember one significant conversation we had about missions:

"I've never felt that overseas missions is for me," he said.

"What do you mean? How can you be sure?" I had at least tried to be open to the possibility myself.

"Because I see such a need for Christians right here," he said. "I believe God has given me a gift of teaching and the desire to work in the university setting. I feel he is impressing it upon me that this is where I should be. Besides, there's also the matter of my health."

"Your health?" I couldn't imagine anything being wrong with him, other than the occasional times he complained about headaches. This guy unleashed furious serves on the tennis court, and power drives on the golf course. "What's wrong with your health?"

"Colitis!" he muttered. "With all the trouble this miserable condition has given me, I'd be a mess in a foreign country."

"Pete, I never knew you had that problem. I always thought it was your headaches that made you feel so awful."

"Unfortunately, that's true too. One doesn't like to talk about these things. I just try to live with it. Maybe the headaches will let up when the pressure of studies is over. But what about you and missions? Remember when you came back from Camp Imadene last summer? You seemed so serious about serving the Lord. Did you have missions in mind?"

"Oh yes—last summer when I hardly wrote to you? Well, it's true I did a lot of serious thinking about my life. I felt such a responsibility to live for God, especially in light of the great needs I saw there. But I didn't really consider missions seriously. I guess I was thinking back to when I was young. I had wanted to go to the Dominican Republic as a missionary. I knew so many missionaries who worked there because they stayed in our home while on furlough. I think that's even why I took Spanish in high school."

"Sure," he teased, "you probably took it because it was the easiest!"

"That's what everyone told me. But actually, even Spanish was so difficult for me to learn that I decided God could never use me overseas."

That was pretty much the extent of our talks about missions. We didn't discuss the subject again for quite some time. He did talk to me about his trips to Portland, Oregon, where he frequently spoke to a Brethren assembly youth group. This assembly was attended by Jim Elliot's family, all of whom Pete knew well. I had never met Jim, who was studying at Wheaton College in Illinois, but I did know his sister, Jane, from church conferences we had attended together. And of course I had met his parents.

Pete seemed to be intrigued by Jim, who apparently had strong opinions on certain issues. For one thing, Jim opposed war on principle and called himself a conscientious objector. He also scorned the modern-day wedding ceremony, and had such a zealous conviction to remain single that most of his friends believed he opposed marriage altogether. Pete had problems with Jim's views in these areas, and talked about them at length with me.

As the months passed I found myself increasingly drawn to Pete. He was so sincere, so intelligent, so committed to the Lord. I realized I had learned much about Scripture from him, and that my hunger to know God had deepened. Our friendship was fortified through the Word of God, and we began to grow together.

Another event took place my senior year which further affected my relationship with the Lord and with Pete. My family, along with a few other families, left the assembly I had grown up in to start a new church north of Seattle. In many ways I felt I was going to a foreign mission field. Even though we didn't move from our house, I had to leave my friends (nearly all of whom I saw through church) and spend much of my time reaching out to a new community of people, most of whom were not churchgoers.

My father was one of the pioneers in this venture, a classic case of church planting from scratch. Our message, and many of our Brethren ways, were foreign to these people. In order to reach them we had to make many changes in the traditional order of meeting, the time for services, the name of the building and the type of hymnbook. The whole experience served to stretch me spiritually and build my personal confidence. Going from door to door inviting people to church frightened me, but I saw God take my feeble efforts and use them to touch people. A woman from one of the first homes I visited soon showed up in church with her husband; they became the first new followers of Christ in our fledgling assembly. I also taught Sunday school.

As the work grew, we solicited more help. Many young people pitched in, especially university students from the various campus Christian groups. (A number of these students later went on to serve in foreign missions.) A vital, growing church was taking shape. Watching God work in people's lives excited me, and for the first time I saw the newfound faith of adults lead to a complete change in their lives. Their eagerness to understand the Bible challenged me to a more vital commitment to Christ. God was also preparing me for the direction my life would take in a few years.

Because of other commitments, Pete did not join me in helping the new church. Some predicted my move would end our friendship; instead, it strengthened it. Away from the scrutiny of our friends, we no longer had to put up with idle youth-group gossip. On the other hand, the distance between our homes forced Pete to be more creative in order to see me. Unable to use the family car for dates, he decided to buy an old car and fix it up himself. Now Pete knew nothing about cars, but he knew some teenagers who did. He hoped that as they taught him about cars, he would get to know them better and be able to share his faith with them.

Between the teenagers and a few men from church, they managed to start the car, but it died on the street near Pete's home. A few days later, Pete found that his car had been towed away, and he didn't have the money to retrieve it. His father and I felt bad for him, because his investment and his hope for mobility were gone. We learned to make the best of the situation, however, taking the bus or borrowing rides from friends so we could get together. We ended up at each other's homes more often, which resulted in our getting to know each other's parents better. We were seldom alone—for instance, I never even saw Pete's bedroom—but we managed to enjoy our time together.

Pete not only had intellectual prowess, but also a good sense of humor—though he tried hard not to be funny at the expense of hurting others. When I graduated from high school, he presented me with a beautifully wrapped gift. I carefully opened it, only to find a box of candy cigars! I knew exactly what the gift referred to and shrieked with embarrassment.

Pete howled with laughter. My unknowing parents merely shook their heads.

Episodes like this showed me that Pete was less narrow in his lifestyle than I had once thought. If anything, I think he was freer in his Christian life than I was, as well as more mature. He often quoted the Scripture passage about all the good things God has given us to enjoy (1 Timothy 6:17), which included music, art, literature, and the beauty of nature. He loved the mountains, and took every opportunity to backpack with his friends and view God's handiwork. Pete believed that spiritual maturity ultimately depended not on what a person did or didn't do, but rather on one's relationship to God and the focus of one's desires.

After my graduation in 1950, I returned to the same Bible camp in Canada as a summer counselor. I realized how much I had grown since my last stint there. This year, I found it much harder to leave Pete, who had enrolled in summer grad courses. I was thinking seriously about him now. We both wrote to each other regularly.

When I got back from camp in August, Pete and I had a significant date. We had gone out with Dave and Bernice again, but instead of listening to music at Pete's house, we ended up taking a walk in a moonlit park. Pete slowed down and let them go ahead of us, I thought, so they could be alone. Actually, Pete wanted to be alone with me. That night, for the very first time, he looked into my eyes, told me he loved me, and kissed me. It was a special, wonderful moment that marked the beginning of a serious courtship—at least on Pete's part. Though he expressed his feelings more openly to me from then on—and I loved it—I wasn't yet ready to reciprocate.

4
AMBIVALENCE

*W*hen I began courses at the University of Washington in the fall of 1950, Pete and I were dating regularly. It felt great to be out of high school and into a level of study closer to Pete's world and interests. We both lived at home, but since the campus stood midway between our houses, it became our meeting place. We got together almost every day, and—for the first time—in a more relaxed atmosphere than in church or on a double date.

In fact, I found the atmosphere to be *too* relaxed at first. The free exchange of ideas that typically occurs on university campuses unnerved me. I knew about Communism through one of my high school teachers, but in college it seemed people were handing out communist literature all the time (just off campus property). Some girls talked about abortion, which was illegal at this time, as the only solution to an unwanted pregnancy. This was frightening to me. Some of the things I heard made me wonder about the morals of some of the professors as well. And some of the things I saw—porno-graphic pictures, for example, that students had conveniently left in the bathrooms—horrified and disgusted me. Somehow my sheltered upbringing hadn't quite prepared me for this.

To help ease the transition, Pete introduced me to Inter-Varsity, which provided me with much-needed support and a Christian perspective. It quickly became a vital part of our campus life. I watched Pete as he led Bible studies and witnessed his positive influence on the students. He also taught a weekly Bible study for the young people at his church, and spoke to other youth groups around Seattle. His life was immersed in his studies and in the teaching of the Word. Meanwhile, I tried to learn all I could—through I-V and in my classes.

At Pete's recommendation, I took my first and only philosophy course with a professor who had been Pete's undergraduate adviser. It was quite a difficult course for me, but I did get to know the professor outside of the classroom. With Pete's help, I came to understand this man and the discipline of philosophy. I also gained more insight into the academic world in which Pete felt so comfortable.

While I grappled with my studies, Pete was writing his master's thesis on *The Confidence Man,* a rather obscure novel by Herman Melville. I had never heard of anything Melville wrote other than *Moby Dick,* but I came to know a lot more about him—and about Pete's literary perceptions—as I typed the rough draft for his thesis. Sometimes I worked from his handwritten notes; other times he'd dictate while I typed.

We relaxed with each other as the year passed, letting university life be our dating life. Besides studying in the library together and going to I-V meetings, we took many walks on the beautiful wooded campus, and canoed around the marshes of Union Bay, which bordered the school on one side. Again at Pete's suggestion, I took courses in golf, tennis, and bowling to fulfill my Phys. Ed. requirement, though I still had no chance of competing with him. I wanted to please Pete, and we had lots of fun together. (At one point my father jokingly asked me if I was taking any *serious* courses at the university.)

I was very much aware that Pete loved me, and suspected that I was falling in love with him, though I didn't tell him directly. I found myself becoming more interested in the things Pete liked, and actually enjoyed most of the new experiences myself. I even took a music appreciation course, but—alas— still found it very difficult to like classical music. Pete tried to be patient with me.

From my standpoint, life was good; my future looked clear and bright. I had adjusted to my freshman year of college. For the next three years, I assumed I'd finish school while Pete pursued a teaching career. As the end of his graduate studies neared, however, questions about his future arose in his mind. One day he shared his concerns with me.

"Here I am about to complete my Master's degree, Olive, and now I'm beginning to wonder about teaching literature. How can I spend my career talking about material that dwells so much on the base part of life? It is so contrary to Christian truth."

His statement surprised me. I had thought literature was one of Pete's greatest loves. "Why has it taken you so long to discover this?" I said.

"It never bothered me until recently. The deeper I get into American literature, the worse the subject matter seems. And on top of it, teaching positions are scarce, and I really need a Ph.D. to teach at the college level. I'm not sure I want to do any further study in literature."

"What about teaching at a Christian school?" I suggested. "You wouldn't have to teach all that decadent stuff there. And you probably wouldn't need a Ph.D. either."

"True, but it defeats the purpose I had for teaching this subject in the first place. I see the need for Christian teachers on the secular campus. It's a real mission field, and I thought God was leading me into this type of ministry."

"Pete, I don't understand how this can happen. You seemed so sure this was what God had for you."

"I know, Olive. I can't believe I have come this far with no clear guidance for the future. I don't feel my studies have been a waste, or that I missed God's leading." But exactly what God was saying, Pete didn't know.

As we prayed together about Pete's future, he began to think about all the experience he had gained in Bible teaching during the past few years. Others began to confirm that he had gifts in this area.

One day he asked me, "How would you like to be the wife of a Bible teacher instead of a college professor?"

He was only half-kidding. Earlier in our courtship he had talked to me about the responsibilities of a college professor's wife—without ever directly stating he had me in mind. I suppose he was obliquely trying to find out if I was interested; nevertheless, I had thought about it. And I had honestly told the Lord that I was willing for whatever He had for me. But a Bible teacher's wife? I wasn't expecting this. I decided to take his question seriously.

"Are you talking about being a Bible teacher full time?"

"Yes, as a matter of fact I am."

"Seems to me that's a major career change," I said. "Where would you teach? Are you thinking about Bible college or Bible school or in the Brethren assemblies?" I thought of the itinerant Bible teachers who had spoken to our assembly.

Pete grew very serious. "I don't know just where this will lead me," he said. "My studies in literature will still be a help, so that is not lost." Then he took my hand and said, "Olive, do you know I love you and believe God has brought our lives together? You haven't told me how you feel about me. Can you see yourself in this kind of life?"

I knew I loved him, but I was afraid to tell him. I had to be sure of his love, because in my mind the next step would be a permanent commitment to each other. I believed that God had brought us together, but now I had something else to think about—being the wife of a Bible teacher. I saw this as a different type of commitment than that of a professor's wife. I still needed time to think and pray.

"Pete, I can't answer you just now."

My words frustrated him, I'm sure, but he seemed content to wait for me to "come around." In the meantime, the pressure to finish his thesis weighed on him. A couple of months later I did come around, and told Pete that I loved him. Our future remained uncertain, however.

The more Pete thought about Bible teaching, the more excited he got. But he began to wonder if he had sufficient training. After seeking advice and evaluating his five years of university study, as well as his training in the assembly, he felt he needed further education.

In late January he told me he was looking into the possibility of seminary in the fall. "My study in Greek at UW was only a beginning," he said, "and I need some brushing up on what I learned. I need Hebrew and theology as well."

His words had barely reached my ears when a scary thought occurred to me: *Seminary—does that mean we'll have to be apart?* But I kept my cool.

"Are you thinking of Dallas Seminary?" I asked, recalling the only seminary I'd heard of.

"Yes, I've thought about it. My uncle and aunt are great supporters of the school and would love for me to go. They've even offered to help me financially if I go there. But I may have to disappoint them. The New Testament prof I want to study under—Dr. Everett Harrison—has left Dallas and now teaches at a new seminary in California—Fuller Seminary."

"At least California sounds a lot closer than Texas. Would this be for a year?" I tried to stay nonchalant.

"It probably would depend on my course of study," he replied. "Usually it takes three years."

"Three years!" I gasped.

"Right. But that's not all. There's another potential option for the next few years. The draft is breathing down my neck. As soon as I receive my Master's, I'm eligible to be drafted into the service. Dad keeps telling me to enlist with the Navy—he doesn't want me in the Army. I can't see that. I would rather take my chances with a two-year stint in the Army than sign my life away for four years. If the draft call comes before I am accepted by the seminary, then I'll accept it as from the Lord."

I could no longer hide my fear. "What are you saying, Pete—that no matter what happens in the fall, seminary or Army, we are looking at a two- or three-year separation? What will that mean for us?" Now that I had declared my love to Pete, the thought of separation frightened me.

"I feel this could be the best thing for us," Pete said, trying to reassure me. "It could be a time of strengthening our Christian commitment and confirming our love for each other." He paused for a moment. "Olive, I'm not ready for marriage yet, and you still have three years left of school. We have been together so much this year and have grown together, but to be this close for another three years while anticipating marriage could be very difficult. We have goals ahead of us to complete before we can think of getting married. If God has brought us together, he won't let us down."

It was the first time Pete had spoken directly to me about marriage. I knew he was serious. Early that spring, we made a private "commitment" to each other, trusting that the Lord would keep us for each other for marriage in three years. We did not announce our commitment to anyone, because we weren't really engaged. A three-year engagement would be too long, and we had too many questions about the future. But we felt certain that God was leading us to marry.

Pete finally completed his thesis, and received his M.A. in June 1951. He then applied to Fuller Theological Seminary, even though he wasn't completely sure of his plans. He could elude the draft by attending seminary, but did not want draft avoidance to be his motivation for going.

Summer began on a good note. Now Pete and I could enjoy time together (after work) without the pressure of my studies and his thesis. And finally we could both speak openly of our love for each other, even if we didn't know exactly where that love would lead us.

As June and July passed, Pete grew increasingly preoccupied about his future. He did not yet feel completely at peace about attending Fuller. He sought advice, but the elders in his assembly gave him little encouragement. The Brethren saw little need for formal theological education. Seminaries often were viewed as institutions that trained pastors for denominations. Since our church did not accept the validity of "pastors," and looked down on the idea of denominations, many questioned Pete's desire to attend seminary.

My father questioned him, too. "I don't understand why you feel you need to go to seminary," he'd say when Pete came to see me. "There is such a need at the secular universities. Why can't you teach on a campus and have a witness at the same time? Think of all the international students that are coming from countries closed to the gospel." Pete tried to explain his viewpoint; in fact, sometimes they talked for most of the evening. But my father's mind was made up.

Against this backdrop of uncertainty, Jim Elliot came onto the scene one Sunday afternoon in mid-July. Friday and Saturday Pete and I had gone backpacking near Mt. Baker with some of our church friends. It was a wonderful getaway, and I had felt so in love with Pete. We were just finishing Sunday dinner with my parents, and sitting back to enjoy a quiet afternoon together, when Jim called. He wanted to stop by and talk to Pete. The call didn't surprise Pete, since he had invited Jim to speak to the young people's group at Pete's assembly that evening about his plans to go to Ecuador.

Until that afternoon, I had never met Jim, though I had seen him from a distance. What I knew and saw of him as a teenager had frightened me. I had never known such an intense young man: He seemed so strong, so self-assured. Once I had seen him shouting out the gospel at a street meeting in Portland, then cornering people and asking them if they were saved.

Pete had been a good friend of Jim and his family. He admired Jim, even though he didn't share all of Jim's strong views. At that time, Jim believed that one should avoid marriage because it took time and energy that should be given to the Lord's service. Pete did not oppose marriage, but he did share some of Jim's fears about marriage responsibilities getting in the way of ministry.

When Jim arrived at the house a few minutes later, he seemed somewhat serious, and wanted to go out with Pete in the car. They ended up talking for most of the afternoon. I thought it odd for Pete to disappear for so long, but passed it off as two old friends getting caught up. Little did I know how significant that conversation was.

That evening, Jim spoke on being a "eunuch" for the gospel's sake. He talked about his call to work as a single man among the Indians of Ecuador. All my knowledge of Ecuador at that point had come through stamp collecting: I knew it was a small South American country with big stamps. I had no idea that primitive, pagan tribes lived there. Jim said he believed in going out two by two, and that since his two friends from Wheaton College whom he had counted on to join him were now married, he was looking for another single fellow to go with him. I had to admit, Jim's forceful speaking style certainly made the less-than-thrilling idea of being a eunuch for Jesus Christ memorable. I thought he would make a marvelous missionary. But that's as far as my mind went.

Pete, however, wasn't the same after Jim left. He grew more and more preoccupied, but wouldn't talk about it. He seemed cold and indifferent to me. Only occasionally did he call, and then said almost nothing on the phone. I couldn't understand what was happening. This was not like Pete. He knew I was unhappy, but he made no effort to resolve the tension.

Several weeks passed. The time I had so anticipated having with Pete before he left for California was slipping away. I hardly saw him at all; he didn't seem to have time to get together. But he did have time for a trip to Portland to see Jim. I also noticed that Pete stopped talking about going to Fuller; yet he didn't appear to have any other plans in mind. Our lines of communication were breaking down. What was wrong? I feared that the love that had been so fresh as we hiked in the mountains only a few weeks before was now gone.

One day in August, Pete called me. An English missionary to Ecuador, Dr. Wilfred Tidmarsh, was speaking at his assembly. Pete wanted me to come and hear him. (Pete had already heard him in Portland the weekend he visited Jim, and had told me how impressed he was.)

"Well, can you give me a ride?" I said, somewhat irritated that he only called to tell me about a church service.

"Sorry, I can't. But you can find a way to get there, can't you?" He knew I had no transportation and that I wouldn't take the bus at night. Yet he kept insisting that I make every effort to get there. He seemed so cold, and it upset me. I didn't go to the service.

I grew more fearful as the days passed. All kinds of

terrible thoughts filled my head about my relationship with Pete coming to an end. Had our "love" simply resulted from being together every day at school, and now that school was over, were things cooling off? Had he only needed me to help him type his thesis, and no longer found me useful? Had he met someone else?

I had been idealistic about love and about the man I was to marry. I had honestly believed that God would show me his choice at the right time, and that He would spare me from the heartaches some of my friends had experienced because of broken engagements. Now it seemed I was becoming a victim of one of my greatest fears: that once I told a fellow I loved him, he would "dump" me.

My parents told me to face the facts: Pete was nice, but now he wanted to get on with his life. The college romance was over. Because he planned to leave the area in September, now was a good time for him to break things off. (Of course, they knew nothing of the commitment Pete and I had made to each other.)

Remarkably, it had never occurred to me during those weeks that Pete was entertaining the possibility of going to Ecuador himself. I had thought he was interested in Jim's plans simply because of their friendship. Over the past year, we had talked about missions often in relation to Pete's brother, Ken, and his wife Helena, who were preparing for missionary work with the Zulus in South Africa. But whenever we talked about our own future, missions never came up. Pete always spoke of the campus as his mission field, and never completely gave up on the idea of someday teaching in a university.

While anxiety over our relationship consumed my days, Pete independently sought God's wisdom for his future. He did not share his feelings with me; instead, he disclosed his new thoughts about missionary service to others. He also corresponded with both Jim and Dr. Tidmarsh. After his August visit with Jim in Portland, Pete wrote him:

> Boy, it was great. . . . I certainly did enjoy my weekend with you, Jim, and it was thoroughly profitable as well. My soul has been filled with rich material for meditation since I returned. The [camaraderie] was really *great*. . . .
>
> The main purpose of this note, Jim, is to urge you to even greater prayer re: my exercise toward Ecuador. Gave a hint of it to Dr. T. and he seemed to have anticipated it and told me of his prayer for a co-laborer for you. Also told me of the warm welcome for me in Ecuador should God so lead. Personally I am much burdened before the Lord about it, though I do not know what God's mind about it is. Brother, beseech God that He will control my thinking about Ecuador. If I know my own heart—and this is always difficult—I am willing to move forward if this be the will of God. Pray, as God impels you to do so!! Any of your thinking on the matter would be of help. Speak your mind, and speak straight if need be. . . .
>
> Let me know soon if we can work out some time together. As you know, both present (i.e. Fuller, etc.) and future plans depend on obtaining the mind of Christ about Ecuador, and going out with you to labor together. A great door . . . many adversaries.

Unknown to me, Pete was about to come to a decision which changed not only his seminary plans, but the entire course of his life, and ultimately mine.

5
SINGLE

*I*n late August of 1951, Pete wrote to Jim:

> [The Lord] has been leading my meditation to the
> stringent statements of Christ regarding discipleship—
> especially those words of Christ to his disciples before he
> sent them out to preach two and two: "He that loveth
> father or mother more than me is not worthy of me." And
> the often repeated key to life—"He that findeth his life
> shall lose it: and he that loseth his life for my sake shall
> find it." I have been directed to these and similar passages
> again and again. I should like to put these truths to the
> utmost test; God, I believe, is honored when we push
> great promises and commands to the greatest possible
> extent. Ecuador has appeared in my mind as an opportu-
> nity to put God to the test—quite in the spirit of Moses in
> Exodus 33. Personal inability and ineptitude demand of
> God that He should perform the impossible for me.
> Seemingly God delights in many instances to place men in
> situations which magnify their weaknesses for the simple
> delight of showing Himself strong to all observers.

Pete had made a life-changing decision in less than a month. He was willing to follow the Lord to the primitive jungles of Ecuador. The very weaknesses that had previously kept him from considering the mission field were now viewed as a proving ground for showing God's strength.

All this time I had remained in the dark about Pete's growing conviction. Without knowing why, I felt I mattered less and less to him. Finally, toward the end of the summer, he called and asked me to spend an afternoon at the beach with him. A date!

I hardly noticed the long bus ride to the church where Pete worked as custodian. I was to meet him there, and then we would hop another bus down to the beach. Pete and I would soon be together. Now all my doubts about his love for me seemed foolish.

When I arrived at the church, Pete was nowhere to be found. I was furious, and my doubts returned. Finally he appeared, but he offered me no kiss or hug for a greeting. He was having prayer with a friend, he said, and wouldn't be ready for an hour. Would I mind waiting?

What could I say? He was praying with someone. Begrudgingly, I waited and fretted. I thought people in love wanted to be together. This was our first date in a month. Who knows? Maybe it would also be our last date before he left for seminary—if indeed he was still headed there. I didn't get it: Once we had declared our love for each other and made a commitment for the future, we seldom talked anymore, and were tense with each other when we did. Maybe Pete's fears had grown about marriage restricting his ministry. I tried to entrust our relationship to God, but found it difficult, since I felt He was somehow responsible for what was happening.

When Pete eventually emerged from his impromptu prayer meeting, we no longer had time for the beach—only for a short talk. So we rode to a closer park overlooking the beach.

As we sat on the bus, I was unhappy and Pete withdrawn. He showed no sign of affection, and gave no apology for cutting short our one and only date of the month. I was so upset by what had happened to our relationship that I didn't care about his decisions about ministry and career. I didn't ask him about his seminary plans. I just made a little small talk and tried to hold myself together; I knew I'd start to cry if I blurted out all my pent-up questions.

We got off the bus and walked for a while in the park. Pete didn't hold my hand, and there was an awkward silence. The late afternoon sun had just begun to drop behind the tall trees. We found a gentle, grassy slope and sat down.

"What has happened to us, Pete?" I said at last. "You seem so different. I don't understand."

Pete finally broke his silence. "Do you remember when I wanted you to hear Dr. Tidmarsh tell of his missionary work in Ecuador?" he began. "It was one of the most incredible missionary stories I had ever heard. I was so impressed with the severity of life in the jungles. I thought that if you had heard about the work in Ecuador, you'd be able to understand what I am about to tell you."

"But Pete, I had no way to get there that night. I remember you did tell me a few things about him on the phone—the primitive way he and his wife had to live, and then about the plane accident she was in."

"Right. Because of that plane accident, they probably will never be able to live in the jungles again. He has been praying for single men for the jungle work."

"And that's where Jim is going, right?"

"Yes, and he has been praying about another single fellow to go with him. He had hoped that two other friends of his at Wheaton would go with him, but they both were married in June."

"So what does this have to do with us?"

Pete took a deep breath and continued. "It is very difficult to tell you this, Olive, but I felt you should know before I talk to the elders at the assembly. I am planning, Lord willing, to go with Jim to Ecuador."

The impact of his words didn't really register. I immediately assumed this was something he was *considering,* something we could discuss together.

"I don't understand," I said. "How long have you been thinking about this? What about your plans for seminary and Bible teaching? What about the mission field you talked about on the university campus? Did Jim's visit last month have anything to do with this decision?"

"I was so uncertain about seminary, and got so little encouragement that I took it as a good indication that the Lord was not leading me there. When Jim visited last month, we did talk about Ecuador and he told me about the need for another single man. I felt that this opportunity came at a time when I was looking for an answer from God about my future. Being single, I fulfill the requirement. I really believe God has led me to this decision."

I still was not sure how this affected our relationship. "Well, how long do you think you would be there?"

"I have no idea. However long it takes to do the work. It could be ten years."

"Ten years! Pete, what about us?"

"Olive, I don't know how to say this, but I don't see any other way. I can't ask you to wait ten years for who knows what. It may be that I will never marry. The work needs to be done by single men who are free from family responsibilities."

The terrible reality was sinking in. He really *had* made a decision. "Are you saying it is over between us?"

"Yes, I'm afraid I am."

Tears filled my eyes. I couldn't believe what I was hearing. He had made a hasty decision, probably because of

Jim. "How could you come to a decision like this without even talking to me?" I protested. "How can you walk out of my life? What about the Lord's will for our lives together? What about our love for each other? What about our commitment? How can you say it is over?"

"We are not breaking an engagement, Olive. No one knows of our commitment, so we won't have to make any explanations."

I could see he had not even considered me. My throat tightened and I began to cry. Obviously I had not meant that much to him after all. Surely he didn't understand all the implications of his decision.

"What about your health?" I said through my tears. "You said before that it was one of the main reasons you wouldn't go overseas. And now you're talking about a primitive jungle situation. What has changed? Certainly not your health."

"You know the verse in 2 Corinthians 12—that God's grace is sufficent for me and his power will be made perfect in my weakness? I believe that will be true for me."

I still wasn't convinced. "What about all the training you've had, and your desire to do Bible teaching?"

"I don't think my going to Ecuador rules out that possibility for the future," he said. "I'm too young and inexperienced to be an effective teacher right now. But in Ecuador I have an opportunity as a young man to serve on the front lines. I must leave my future in teaching with the Lord."

Okay, so he had sorted out the teaching issue. But why hadn't he considered my going to Ecuador with him?

"There is another uncertainty about my future," Pete continued, addressing my unspoken question. "Jim told me about some unreached tribes in Ecuador—the Aucas and the Cofanis. The Aucas are known killers. If God is calling Jim and me to reach those people, we must stay single. These tribes haven't been located yet, and we have no idea how long it will take to find them. That's why I can't ask you to wait indefinitely for me."

I could not imagine him in a place like this. "Pete, you have spent your whole life in books. How will you ever survive in the jungles?"

"Going with Jim will help. He has all the practical know-how and I can learn from him. I am convinced God has brought us together for this work."

I sat there in stunned silence. I had run out of arguments. Pete was utterly serious about Ecuador—and about breaking up with me.

Then came the final blow. "Olive," Pete said, "I don't think we should see each other again. It would just prolong the agony. I think it would be best to make a clean break and not even write. Time is short, as I will be leaving as soon as I get a commendation from the elders to go to Ecuador. Then I have to meet Jim out East in a month to speak in several assemblies. Jim hopes to leave for Ecuador by the end of the year. I'm trusting that my visa will come so that, Lord willing, I can leave with him. So I guess this is good-bye."

"What about our plans for the Labor Day conference?"

"I'll still be going with Ken and Helena, but I think it would be very awkward for us if you went. I'll be staying with Jim in Portland."

It was over. Just like that. My mind reeled with a million things I wanted to say to Pete, but none that would make any difference. Without another word, I jumped up and ran out of the park to find the bus. I had to get out of there, away from Pete. Luckily the bus was waiting, and I got right on.

The sun glistening on the waves of Puget Sound always made me squint when I looked out over the water late in the day. But today, looking out the bus window, my own tears blinded me. I was devastated. I felt overwhelmingly rejected. During the half-hour ride home, I replayed in my head all the things Pete had told me. Evangelism and missions and jungles and Indians didn't concern me at that point. All I could think about was what had happened to me. How could God have allowed it, after he had brought Pete and me together?

I couldn't pray; I didn't know how to pray about this situation. Pete's friends had told him a year ago that I wasn't the one for him. If we had listened to them then, or if Jim had come into Pete's life back then, I would not have been hurt like this. We were friends then, and we could have remained friends. But instead, we became romantically involved and made a commitment to each other which had to be broken. Now we couldn't even be friends.

I knew it must have been difficult for Pete to say what he did, but why did he have to be so cold and unfeeling about it? He could have taken me in his arms and told me how much he loved me, or he at least could have told me he was sorry his plans had changed. But he didn't. He simply recited the hard facts of how God had led him into a whole new ministry. But even if he did do a clumsy job of breaking the news to me, should I not accept his decision and be grateful that God had answered his prayers? No, it wasn't that easy, I told myself. I had been a vital part of those prayers before. Now Pete was claiming he had found God's "perfect will" for his life, with no thought (or at least no discussion) of its implications for me.

The more I thought about Pete's decision, the more convinced I was that Jim had talked Pete into it. It had all happened too quickly. Jim, so sure of God's will for his life, simply expected that his friends would join him on the mission field "where the need was so great."

As far as I knew, I would never see Pete again. I was so hurt and angry by that point that I didn't care. I simply wanted to erase all memory of that afternoon. The bus finally arrived at my stop, and I got off. At least the ride had given me enough time to pull myself together before I faced my parents.

The hurried decision Pete had made was out of character for the Pete I knew. He knew little about the work beyond what Jim and Dr. Tidmarsh had told him. All he seemed to know was that singleness was a prerequisite. Dr. Tidmarsh himself had begun the work among the jungle Indians as a single missionary. When he married, he had brought his wife back with him and they had lived very primitively. On one of Mrs. Tidmarsh's flights to the jungle, the plane had crashed and she was so badly injured that Dr. Tidmarsh had to abandon the jungle work. His conclusion? The rigors of jungle living were too difficult for a woman. So he began looking for young single men like Jim—and now Pete—to reopen the station, which he had named Shandia.

Meanwhile, Jim wrote back to Pete:

> I have no word for you re: Ecuador. I would certainly be glad if God persuaded you to go with me. But *He* must persuade you. How shall they preach except they be *sent*? If the Harvest-Chief does not move you, I hope you remain at home. There are too many walls to leap over not to be fully persuaded of God's will.[1]

The intensity of my doubt and despair increased over the next few days. I dared to question how God could have misled us so completely. How could we discount more than two years of friendship, fellowship, prayer, sharing, and finally loving? Pete's announcement made me wonder how we could even know the difference between God's will and our own will. Had God truly led us together, or did we only use those words to reassure ourselves that we were doing the right thing?

I had believed Pete when he told me he loved me and believed God was leading us together. We had grown together over many years. Now Pete felt we had been mistaken—that God had opened a door for him and he had to respond, regardless of prior commitments. If Pete was so sure God was leading him in a different way, why hadn't God also led *me* to the same conclusion? I just couldn't believe he could set aside our life-commitment to each other just because of something he experienced over one month's time. Either Pete had never really loved me, or God's leading and human love had nothing to do with each other.

In his letter back to Jim, Pete wrote: "Ecuador has seemed an answer in life to God's severe demands on his disciples. . . . missionary life in Ecuador is severe enough an answer, on a material level, to the severity and self-sacrifice implicit in Christ's declarations." The "severe demand" on Pete apparently included the need to sever any earthly ties that would hinder his service. My question was: Did he take this step of faith on his own, in response to what he saw as God's will for his life, or had he been unduly influenced by others?

6
OBLIGATION

On August 28, 1951, a few days after Pete told me of his decision, he wrote to Jim:

> . . . the challenge has come at a time when I am waiting upon God for leading—my path was not fully clear and my pointing toward Fuller tentative. This may be the open door as to "where" that I have been praying about for years.
>
> The work there involves going out two and two—a thoroughly Biblical and sensible means of stepping out. Also, along this line, God has brought our paths together in a way not anticipated or planned, and the thought of working together in Ecuador could not be the result of collusion or simply the attraction of personalities.
>
> If I am to go to Ecuador it must be that God alone persuades me, and therefore I am glad that He has given a maximum of exercise and, up till now, a minimum of planning together. I am very thankful that you have not persuaded me in any way to come with you; God has led you in this. As you say it *must* be His persuasion. But if it

is His, and He does persuade, it is great to know that going out together is the Harvester's divine pattern. . . .

The work demands single men who are free to remain single for some time, and I am in this position. Until recently I was *under some obligation* [italics added]—I will tell you more about this when I see you and have more space and time—but I am now free to consider any field as a single man. Should God indicate that I am to make myself a eunuch for the kindgom of heaven's sake I am grateful, and look on it as a privilege: Isaiah 56:4–5.

Here was the bare fact: I was an "obligation" from which Pete thought he should be free. He may have thought that talking about "the Lord's leading" or "God's will" would soften the blow. But there was no way around it. Pete's demands on himself had led him to disown me and my love. My suspicions had been true. In response to that rejection, I blamed God for misleading us. I also blamed Jim Elliot for unduly influencing Pete—not necessarily with direct persuasion, but with his forceful personality.

I continued to hope that Pete would realize he had made a mistake. But the days went by and I heard nothing from him. My parents, who had liked Pete and had never discouraged our relationship, hated to see me so distraught. They thought that perhaps I had misunderstood his intentions earlier. They didn't know the whole story, but they still supported and empathized with me.

Meanwhile, Pete became more convinced than ever that God was indeed leading him in this direction. Apparently the idea of working in Ecuador had charged him with a new sense of purpose—had given him a challenge he could pursue with "abandon" (a term Jim used). The way he adopted Jim's strong word "eunuch" and depersonalized me as an "obligation" in his letter show how intense that sense of purpose was. He viewed me as the one thing that stood in the way of his total commitment to serving the Lord.

Although Pete had clearly told me he was going to Ecuador, he apparently had not come to a complete decision. In the same letter, Pete told Jim, "Crystal clear certainty is not yet mine, but I am waiting much upon God and rest on the knowledge that you are doing the same. I feel that if God led us to labor together He would seal me to your heart, and that to that extent you will share in my leading. Let's give ourselves to prayer!"

"God sealed our hearts together." "Sharing in my leading." Pete had used those identical phrases with me during all those months we had prayed together about *our* future—even after we had anticipated a separation of several years. Exactly why Pete felt he could dispense with me and transfer this language about God's will to Jim was never quite clear. Did he feel compelled to make a clean break with me in order to prove to God he meant business? Did he need to show Jim that he could be counted on, and would not leave him stranded in Ecuador in order to get married? Or did he truly view his decision as a disciple's acceptance of God's demands? However Pete saw it, from my human perspective I concluded that Jim had convinced him that he needed to remain single in order to serve God. I was expected to accept this as God's will.

(I should say here that I never saw the above letter from Pete to Jim until I found it twenty-five years later. Its stark reference to my being an "obligation" came as a shock even after all those years. But it did confirm that my suspicions at that time were real. Had I known then that he had written these words to Jim, I probably would have walked out of his life forever that day in the park.)

Within a week of his announcement to me, Pete met Jim in Portland for the Brethren Labor Day Conference. Although he had suggested that I not go, I went anyway with some of my friends. I stayed clear of him, as he wanted, but I did see him from a distance. I expected him to be happy and excited, since God had revealed his future to him; instead he seemed pretty sober. I certainly was.

During the conference Pete talked at length with Jim about Ecuador. Afterward, on September 6, he wrote to Dr. Tidmarsh, summarizing the chain of events leading to his decision:

> Since your visit, and even just a little before it, Jim and I have been in constant correspondence over the exercise of mine regarding Ecuador, and so last weekend [Labor Day] we had the chance to talk it over together. We confirmed a number of decisions which we had arrived at independently. . . .
>
> Until about a year ago my thinking about the Lord's service was more in terms of Bible teaching here at home.

He went on to describe the various Bible classes he had taught for Inter-Varsity and at his assembly.

> All these, plus many other less permanent responsibilities, led me to think that *perhaps* God was preparing me for this type of ministry, and was using my education to quicken my mind and sharpen my mental tools in preparation for it. But about a year ago I became especially exercised about the foreign field, just at the time when my brother felt confirmed in his going out to South Africa. I devoured all the missionary books and magazines I could find. . . . I became exercised about South and Central America and collected as much prayer material as possible about the missionaries in these lands. I particularly followed in prayer your own needs and activities. . . .

He mentioned his consideration of seminary, and then continued:

At any rate I have been waiting on the Lord about my future, expecting Him to open the door to the place where He wanted me whenever it pleased Him to do so.

Jumping ahead to early this summer, he said:

It was at this time that I heard from Jim after a lapse of correspondence, and though he mentioned almost nothing about Ecuador in the letter, and certainly nothing about my being concerned about Ecuador, I felt compelled to pray then and following about the possibility of my also going to Ecuador. In mid-July Jim came up to Seattle for a weekend, and at that time he mentioned the need of single young men in Ecuador and asked me to pray about it, though of course he applied no pressure *at all.* . . .

I felt at that time in our contact together, and in seeing the pictures of the work there, that perhaps God was calling me to join Jim as a co-laborer, since I knew of his earnest desire to find a young fellow like himself to go with him, and since I felt a freedom to go if God should definitely indicate. But I wanted to make sure that all my exercise was of God and not just the product of a set of circumstances. Thus I said nothing of it while there, and even said little to Jim of it, except that we covenanted to labor in prayer about it that nothing be done hastily and without the clear seal of God's approval. . . . I am free to go, and have the desire to do so.

Pete not only picked up information about Ecuador at the Labor Day conference. He also learned something interesting about Jim: he had not severed his ties with Betty Howard, a young woman he had met and dated at Wheaton. Pete noticed a picture of her in Jim's bedroom. Jim acknowledged that he still cared for Betty, but explained that marriage was out of the question as she was going to Africa and he to Ecuador. This new information must have startled Pete, especially since he had just finished telling Jim that he had dispensed with his own "obligation."

A few days after the conference, to my surprise, Pete called me. I never expected to hear from him again. We talked about the conference. I didn't particularly enjoy hearing about his time with Jim, but I listened anyway. Then he told me about Betty's picture.

"Hmm," I said. "Is she the girl who visited him two years ago? I remember everyone was surprised that Jim had a girl. Is he going with her?" I couldn't quite reconcile this with Jim's speech about being a eunuch.

"Yes, it's the same girl," Pete replied. "He said he cares for her very much, but because he is going to Ecuador and she to Africa, there is no future for them. He plans to see her when he is speaking out East and will settle their relationship." Pete seemed to feel that Jim was breaking it off with Betty.

After that phone call, I wondered if Pete was having second thoughts about our relationship. His unexpected discovery about Jim and Betty had affected him strongly enough to break his silence and talk to me about it. I wondered why Jim hadn't said a word about Betty before. And I thought it strange that Jim did not say he couldn't marry Betty because he was committed to a single life, but rather because she was going to Africa.

Our conversation made me more sure than ever of Jim's influence on Pete—if not by overt pressure, certainly by Jim's very strong conviction. Now Pete was seeing another side of Jim. Was it causing him to rethink my place in his life? I never asked him.

7
MIXED SIGNALS

I never knew exactly when Pete's father learned of the news, but I heard it upset him a great deal. He was already "losing" one son, Ken, to the mission field, but Ken had been planning and preparing for missions over the past several years. To think of his other son going overseas at the same time, especially on such short notice, distressed him. Having heard about the primitive, rigorous life of the jungles, he could not imagine Pete surviving there with his health problems. Pete had spent all of his life in school, reading books; he was a thinker, not the jack-of-all-trades one needs to be in an uncivilized culture.

He desperately tried to dissuade his son from going, using the same arguments I had—health, gifts that didn't match the assignment, the sudden change of direction, and so on. Knowing that Pete would be seeking the commendation of the elders at the assembly, his father even went to some of them to express his concerns. He strongly believed that Jim had influenced Pete, because he had seen how much Pete had changed after Jim's visit.

At one point I was able to talk briefly with Pete's father. I had no idea what Pete had told him about our relationship, or if he knew that Pete had broken up with me. He certainly knew something had happened, because he never saw us together.

"My son has changed," he told me bluntly, "and I think Jim is responsible. He talked Pete into going to Ecuador."

Pete's decision had hurt him partly because he had different hopes for his son. But Pete's treatment of me bothered his father even more than it did my own parents. He reacted in the same way: "You have got to forget Pete and get on with your life." With both sets of parents believing that Jim had unduly influenced Pete, I felt all the more sure that it was true.

In spite of his father's protests, and mine, Pete tried to move forward with his next step toward Ecuador, which was obtaining a "commendation" from the elders of his assembly. The Brethren have a service agency, Christian Missions in Many Lands, but it does not function as a mission board. This agency doesn't choose the missionaries. Each assembly assumes full spiritual responsibility for anyone going overseas. Therefore, the elders must firmly believe that God is leading each candidate. They carefully interview the person, looking for sufficient evidence of a godly life and gifts in the required areas of ministry. While commendation is not the same as ordination, it is given only to those who they believe are called to full-time ministry. (Most young people will talk to the elders about their "exercise," or desire, to do the Lord's work long before their place of service is known, so that by the time commendation is officially sought, the elders are not surprised. Even then, however, they may ask candidates to serve in the local church for a year to prove their calling and to test their gifts.)

After his first meeting with the elders, Pete gave Jim the following report:

> The situation regarding Ecuador looks encouraging. When I got back [from Portland] last Wednesday I mentioned my exercise to the brethren following the

prayer meeting. They seemed somewhat taken aback, but most of them seemed interested and pleased. I asked them to pray about commending me to the work there after I had described it. . . . In as wise a way as possible I suggested that it would be helpful if they could make a decision speedily, i.e. as speedily as the nature of the thing permits.

Their speed surprised everyone, including me. They called a meeting on Monday . . . there was a two hour discussion about the Biblical basis. . . . To summarize the rambling and, at times, animated discussion, the brethren decided to meet again next Monday for a final decision. Most of the brethren were willing to commend me then at that meeting, but a few were hesitant—thus the delay. The hesitancy was over a disagreement which arose about whether I had the health and physical stamina to stand the rigors of jungle life, and whether I was capable to stand life in the rough. Most felt that the Lord would give the grace and strength if he had given the call, but some felt that a little rugged preparation here in the homeland would be wise before going. Apparently there would have been no question about commending me if the field to which I felt called had been a semi-civilized one; it was the extremes of Ecuador which made them wonder. . . . They did advise me to write Fuller that I would not be coming this year. All of this I take as from the Lord. . . .

The elders remembered Dr. Tidmarsh's description of life in the jungles and worried that Pete, with his physical limitations, would collapse under the stressful demands of jungle living. The fact that his primary skills were mental rather than practical caused further concern. The elders had to satisfy themselves that Pete would not simply bury his gifts in the jungles of Ecuador.

Pete had hoped to meet Jim in Chicago to strategize and speak at several assemblies, but the elders in Seattle wanted another meeting with him, so he planned to meet Jim later in New Jersey. Timing was becoming critical: he still had to apply for a visa, and might have to wait months for it to be processed. It might not arrive by the first of the year, when Jim had planned to sail.

In spite of the questions people raised about Pete's decision, his brother, Ken, and many of his friends supported him with prayer and encouragement. Some of them even suggested that he leave for Ecuador without the elders' commendation. They thought it was a tremendous opportunity and admired him for deciding to follow the Lord regardless of the cost. In Pete's assembly, some strongly opposed his going. Others trusted his judgment completely.

Pete's friend David Dye later described what he thought was going on in Pete's head at that time:

> He could have said that since God had called him, he had to go, with or without his assembly's approval—which would have been disregarding the fact that God's will must be done in God's way. Or he could have decided that perhaps God had not called him, as some of the elders seemed to believe for a time, and could have dropped the whole matter—which would have been disregarding the fact that a Christian's aim is to please God, not men. Amid lots of poor advice from both impetuous young and visionless old, he kept his balance.[1]

I still believed Pete was making a mistake, and somewhat selfishly hoped that the elders would refuse him the commendation. They finally gave Pete their support and blessing, however. In the end, they couldn't deny this twenty-two-year-old man's dedication or his love for the Lord. And they decided they couldn't say no to someone who was trying to obey God's call in spite of seemingly impossible demands. Pete believed that God would help him overcome every obstacle. Now that the church had given its approval, he could pray with even more confidence that God would deliver his visa on time.

Pete had made several major decisions in a very short time: to pursue missions and specifically Ecuador, to abandon his seminary plans, to remain single, and to dismiss me. He felt so sure he had heard God's call that he moved quickly to clear away all the obstacles. He wanted to obey God, clear and simple.

On his visit with Jim in New Jersey, however, Pete would soon learn that God's call may not have been as clear and simple as he had thought.

In order to understand what Pete was about to experience, it is necessary to provide some background about Jim and his relationship to Betty Howard. In his early years at Wheaton College, Jim had gained the reputation of being a "woman-hater . . . because of his determination to eliminate the nonessentials from his schedule. Dating he regarded as one thing he might well do without. Furthermore . . . God had spoken to him through the word of Matthew 19:12, 'There are eunuchs who have made themselves eunuchs for the sake of the kingdom of heaven.' "[2] His desire to go into tribal work in the jungles of South America, which grew as he continued his studies, had been "settled" at the first Urbana student missions convention in December 1948:

> My decision was based on seeing a man from central Brazilian jungles who has done a work comparable to the sort I feel exercised for. He told of the impossibility of marriage in his particular context. That was all—no voices, no Scripture, just the settled peace of decision which often comes to the exercised soul. I will not say God

is leading me to a life of celibacy. *I only know what I need to know for now,* and that is that the Lord does not want me seeking a wife until I have His definite sign. And apparently there is no immediate reason to expect that sign.[3]

He had made his decision, but also had found himself struggling—almost to the point of martyrdom—with his love for Betty. He had come to know her during his junior year. In the spring of 1948 he had told her of his love, although he did not know if he would ever marry. He had been "confident" that God was leading him to the jungle as a single man, but had not yet received "His definite sign" regarding a wife.

> Because of heartsearching I had had regarding God's use of those who have made themselves eunuchs for the kingdom's sake, I determined that none should know of my affinity for that girl, even though it was evident that we should be much together. I can remember confessing to the Lord what I called "my love for her," and striving daily to forget and swallow hard. In those days of decision to keep silence, it seemed as if I had sealed the course of my whole life, and I must confess, I felt as if I were somewhat of a martyr.[4]

Soon after Jim had declared his love to Betty, he wrote in his journal, "Came to an understanding at the Cross with Betty last night. Seemed that the Lord made me think of it as laying a sacrifice on the altar. She has put her life there, and I almost felt as if I would lay a hand on it, to retrieve it for myself, but it is not mine—wholly God's."[5] Jim's entry on June 15: "Wept myself to sleep last night after seeing Betty off at the depot. Wistful all day today in spite of outdoor exercise. Feel a concentrated pressure in my throat even now. Homesickness partly—but I never felt it until after I left her."[6] At this point,

Betty was planning to go to Africa as a missionary, and Jim to South America. Later Betty's attention shifted to the South Sea Islands.

In September of 1949, Betty had traveled to Portland to visit Jim during a Brethren conference. That was the first time any of Jim's friends, including Pete, had ever heard of her. Since Pete and I had heard of Jim's convictions about marriage, we were astounded to learn he had a girlfriend.

Jim's journal reveals more about how strong his feelings for her were during that visit: "Very intimate with Betty in speaking of our relation. . . . Startled to find ourselves talking about marriage so offhandedly last eve."[7]

When she left Portland, he wrote:

> She has been gone just one hour. What thunders of feeling I have known in that short time. . . . Leaving her is terrible. . . . For it seems each time I see her she wants an answer, some assurance, some little promise for the future. And rightly so. But each time I have no word, only that I must wait. How long? For what? I know not. O God of my bitter moments, Father of Christ who wept, grant me some guidance directly from Thee. May I ask it in Spirit-spawned *faith*, Lord? *Please let us not part again in silence.* I would rather never see her again than have to put her through this "going into silence." Her uprightness makes it so hard. She loves, I know, but, oh, how bitter is love unexpressed. And she will not let me hold her, hardly touch her, for she says, "I am not mine to give you." If God gave her to me and it were certain, if we dwelt not in *silence* but in assurance that He were granting us to one another, it would be easier. She would relax her vigil, and we might embrace. But she does not, and I know how much she longs for light and thence for love."[8]

Amid their own uncertainty, Jim and Betty also had to endure the evaluation of friends and family. Betty was definitely under scrutiny. Their conclusion? "Betty made a poor impression on the family," Jim wrote. "Apparently none feels she fits me, yet we together alone seem to strike if off wonderfully well. But before others she is aloof."[9] The family's opinion further compounded their confusion.

It was a difficult and wonderful relationship. Jim wrote of those days as, "Strange, but oh, such happy days! Were these not of Thee my God? And wilt Thou deny fruition to such love as we have known?"[10] Betty needed the assurance of marriage from Jim. Jim was looking for some expression of her love. On the other hand, he loved her but didn't know if he would ever marry.

From the fall of 1949 until 1951, Jim wrote very little in his journal about Betty, although they remained in contact. In 1950 Jim had learned of the need for missionaries in Ecuador, and had felt that God was leading him there. Outwardly he had appeared to have settled the question of being single. Whenever he had spoken to churches or to his friends, he had communicated that he clearly knew God's will and was following it joyfully.

His journals show otherwise. Jim had kept his love for Betty, and his inner struggle about singleness, a close secret. This explains why Pete had been so surprised to learn that Jim still cared for Betty.

The week before Pete's visit to Jim in New Jersey in fall 1951, Pete thought that Jim was breaking up with Betty. Actually, Jim had come to realize that his desire for Betty might be greater than his conviction to remain single. Rather than saying good-bye, Jim reiterated his strong feelings for her. At her home in Moorestown, New Jersey, he wrote,

Came to settled rest about Betty. I love her. The problem
from now on is not "whom should I marry?" but "should
I marry?" Nearer to her now than ever, yet more
confident still that God is leading me away from her to
Ecuador with Pete, and she to the South Seas. . . .
Discovered later that this contact was terribly upsetting to
her. She wept Sunday and came to peace on Monday.[11]

This is the context in which Pete traveled to New Jersey,
brimming with excitement that his future was now clear. He
was going to Ecuador, and things appeared to be coming
together fast. Various Brethren assemblies in the greater New
York City area had scheduled speaking engagements for them.

He was in for a shock when he arrived. Jim was staying at
Betty's home, at her request. Not only were they still seeing
each other, but their relationship was stronger than ever.

Jim wrote in his journal that he was hesitant to stay with
Betty, "as it will complicate things and provide some embarrassment since Pete is already expecting me. Guide me, Lord, let
me miss no path I must walk to deal justly . . . . she had told her
parents the news of our desire and intention, under God, of
marriage."[12]

A few days later, Jim, Betty, her brother Phil, and his
wife, Margaret, picked up Pete and headed for Franconia
Notch in New Hampshire for a few days. As they hiked and
enjoyed the scenery, Pete realized that Jim and Betty were more
than casual friends—they were deeply in love. He could also
tell they were both struggling over having to say good-bye
shortly. Watching two couples in love amid the splendor of the
mountains made Pete feel like the odd man out.

At about this time I received my first truly personal letter
from him. He was actually missing me! The letter said
something to this effect:

You would love it here. Our days have been filled with the enjoyment of nature. However, sitting around in the evenings it is different. The two couples have each other and I feel like a "fifth wheel." Jim and Betty are having a hard time with the thought of saying goodbye for who knows for how long. Jim tells me that he is not sure of Betty's love because she can't tell him and there is no physical expression.

I wondered why Pete told me this, when he obviously could not tell me he loved me anymore or show any affection. I was getting mixed signals.

I didn't answer his letter right away. I still felt afraid and bitter about the whole mess. I believed Pete had written me only out of loneliness and confusion. Then another letter arrived. And another. Pete seemed to miss me, but I could sense no significant change from that day in August. Each letter only plunged me deeper into despair.

One day I received a copy of a newsletter Pete had sent to his parents. I read that a couple by the name of Bill and Irene Cathers was going to Ecuador with Pete and Jim. Bill had attended the Summer Institute of Linguistics with Jim in the summer of 1950, where they first heard about Dr. Tidmarsh's jungle work in Ecuador and of the unreached Auca Indian tribe. During that summer, Jim had come to believe that God was directing him also to work among those Indians. He had hoped that Bill would join him as a single man, but Bill married Irene in June 1951. Nevertheless, the Cathers decided they still wanted to go. The letter also mentioned another unnamed married couple who intended to serve in Ecuador.

Here was yet another twist. Pete breaks up with me because jungle work requires single men. Then Jim gets together with Betty, and now a married couple, possibly two couples, announce they're going with Jim and Pete. The more I tried to understand the leading of God, the more confused I became.

At the bottom of the newsletter Pete had scribbled a short note to me: "I have found out more about the work in Ecuador, but I will wait until I get home to tell you. I am giving you the address of the next stop. I hope you will write. I am looking forward to hearing from you." Apparently Pete was doing some rethinking about his future.

My letter back to him was somewhat guarded, but full of questions. Pain and confusion kept me from sharing my real feelings of love with him. I couldn't allow myself to be hurt again.

But I did begin to wonder if Pete was trying slowly to mend our relationship. What was the new information he had learned? If the Cathers were going, there obviously must be a place for couples in the jungle. It crossed my mind that perhaps Pete would eventually ask me to join him in Ecuador. I had to think seriously about how I'd respond. I found it terribly hard to distinguish between my own feelings of love for Pete and what God really wanted for me—if indeed they were different. Could I expect God to give me guidance independently from Pete? I was far too young to go to the mission field as a single woman; I had no training and no apparent gifts that would especially suit me for jungle work.

Meanwhile, Jim's struggle with singleness continued. Back at home in Portland, on November 20, 1951, he wrote in his journal:

> I began last night to consider engagement with Betty. Frightens me to think of finally leaping over all the old barriers I've raised against marriage. Is it to be, after all, the conventional life of rugs and appliances and babies? Is Paul's example of single intensity beyond me? Am I at last not one of those who make themselves eunuchs for the

Kingdom of heaven's sake? I feel no bitterness, but a sense of regret at losing all the good liberties God has allowed me until now, should I make the promise. No settlement in my mind one way or another though I feel strongly that for my own stability, for Betty's ease, and for most folks' tongues, I should buy a ring. . . .

Lord, which way? "Thou hast heard the desire of the meek: Thou wilt prepare their heart" (Ps. 10:17). What shall I say to all the liberty I've been given to preach adherence to Pauline method—even to single men working on the field and illustrating it from Pete's intention and my own? Rather, what will men think who have heard me say, "I go single, in the will of God" when, if I were really engaged, my plans would be otherwise? Well, it is in God's hands. He gave direction to speak that way. And after all, an engaged man is still single, but purposing to be married. And Paul would have me free from care . . . did he ever love a woman?[13]

In Jim's mind at this point, love and the will of God almost appeared to be subordinate to emotional stability and the opinions of others—to the point that he had to rationalize engagement as being "still single." Surely Jim's mixed feelings, and the mixed signals he had communicated, had their effect on Pete. Perhaps they challenged Pete to be a little less dogmatic about the mysteries of God's will. But I still didn't know where that left me.

8
SEPARATION

*S*hortly after Pete broke up with me in August 1951, I began my second year at the University of Washington. Fortunately, the busyness of studies kept me from focusing too much on my pain. But at the same time, I found myself thinking and studying more about Ecuador. I just had to understand why this country was so important to Pete that he could give up teaching, seminary, and me to go there. I also wanted to learn anything I could about the Auca Indians. In my anthropology course, for example, I wrote a research paper on the South American Indians of the Amazon Basin. To my horror, I learned that the white men who first explored the jungles in search of rubber trees had brutalized and murdered Indians all along the way. Other than this gruesome bit of history, my research turned up almost nothing about any of the Indian tribes, and no mention of the Aucas whatsoever. Writing the paper served to pique my curiosity, however.

In October, my parents took a trip to the Midwest, stopping to see their friends, the McCullys, in Wisconsin. There they learned a surprising piece of news: the McCullys' son, Ed, and his wife, Marilou, were preparing for missions work in

Ecuador. Ed and Marilou turned out to be the other married couple Pete had mentioned in his newsletter. The McCullys, too, worried that Jim Elliot had unduly influenced Ed's decision. This revelation only strengthened my parents' belief that Jim had swayed Pete.

I had not known before that Ed was the other single man from Wheaton (along with Bill Cathers) that Jim had wanted on his Ecuador team. Now both Ed and Bill had married, yet both were still going to Ecuador. How incredible this all seemed. Was God indeed working, I wondered, or was Jim's strong personality still controlling these young men?

Jim's journal gives more background on his part in Ed's life. Ed had been attending law school when, in the fall of 1950, he had written to Jim. His priorities had changed. He had decided to "quit school and begin looking for open doors for a sold-out life."[1] A month later (October 18) Jim had written:

> Yet I feel constrained to go to Milwaukee to seek Ed McCully, much the same as Barnabas went to Tarsus to seek Saul long ago. Lord, I have trust in Thee with all my heart and now confess that I have no understanding upon which I can lean. Grant that my way may be prepared before me . . . . Do the first work there of knitting Ed and me . . .[2]

On October 24, from Ed's home, he had written:

> Praying for guidance for Ed regarding the Lord's work in Ecuador. . . . I sense crisis for Ed and the danger of influencing him wrongly, so grant me wisdom in all that I say among the family here.[3]

In January 1951 Ed joined Jim in a pioneering ministry in Chester, Illinois. He had met Marilou a couple of months prior to going, and they were engaged while he was in Chester. In June 1951—a week after the Cathers were married—

Ed married Marilou. Only a few weeks after these weddings, Pete had "heard from Jim after a lapse of correspondence." When Ed's and Bill's marriages eliminated them as potential single partners (though not as married missionaries), Jim had quickly turned to Pete.

When Pete returned in November from his New Jersey visit with Jim, he had much preparing to do for the field. Miraculously, his visa had arrived in record time, enabling him to leave for South America with Jim, and confirming to him that God was indeed leading him.

I had fantasized of a grand reunion with Pete, complete with tears, forgiveness, and plans for our future. That didn't happen, but at least we got together to talk about Ecuador. Finally I could hear more about what had happened out East, and find out about this new member of the team who was married.

Pete came to my home one afternoon. He was friendly, but acted more like a "buddy" than he did the man who had talked marriage with me only a few months before. It reminded me of when we first dated. After some small talk, I got right to the point.

"So, after all you've said about jungle work being only for single men, how is it this couple is going with you and another couple later?"

Pete explained the latest plan. "As soon as we master Spanish, Jim and I will head for the jungles to reopen the Shandia station—the one that's been closed since Mrs. Tidmarsh's accident. Once that is underway, a couple can live there and take over the work, leaving Jim and me free for the itinerant work in the jungles."

"In other words, you found out that life there is not as bad as you first heard and led me to believe."

"Yes, I suppose you could say that," he said, trying not to be defensive. "But it still has not changed my own conviction that there is a lot of work that can only be done by single men. How long it will take to accomplish some of our goals, God only knows."

"So your future is as uncertain as it was before?"

"Right, and because of that I can't ask you to wait for me. I believe it's possible that marriage is in my future. I just have no idea when."

"Pete, when we talked about marriage last summer you weren't sure then how long it would be, but you still believed that the Lord had brought us that far together and that he would not let us down. Why is this so different?"

"This is far more uncertain than my plans for teaching seemed to be," he said. "I just don't know what we will be facing down there. I can't give you any hope for the future until I know for myself. I don't plan to spend all my life in jungle work—perhaps I can think about marriage then. But right now I don't know how long that will be. I believe, ultimately, that I will be a Bible teacher, but I need to prove myself. Like Paul said to Timothy: 'But watch thou in all things, endure afflictions, do the work of an evangelist, make full proof of thy ministry.'* The work in Ecuador, from what I know, will fulfill these requirements for me. I am confident that God has directed me to go."

The message came through loud and clear, but with a few changes. Pete had ruled out neither marriage nor Bible teaching. But he made no promise that I would ever fit into his future. Every signal I received indicated that God was leading him away from me and into this new work. As we sat there in my living room, I wondered if he was waiting for me to say I believed that God was calling me to Ecuador, too. Maybe he felt he couldn't say anything about his feelings for me until I had reached that decision on my own.

*2 Timothy 4:5 KJV.

Pete's voice brought me out of my musings. He was telling me of yet another unexpected development.

"There's a possibility that two single girls will be joining us some time next year," he said. "One is Jim's girlfriend, Betty Howard, and the other is Dorothy, a girl who has been working at the *Voices of the Vineyard** office."

"Really? I thought Betty was going with a South Seas mission."

"Those plans fell through, so she is free now to go to Ecuador. I don't know who they will work with or what Dorothy's skills are. I do know that Betty is gifted linguistically. Between her language training and her background in Greek from Wheaton, she will be a great asset in translation work."

It all sounded pretty fishy to me. "So, Betty is going now? What ever happened to Jim being a eunuch?" I knew there was more to Jim and Betty's relationship than they were admitting, and I wondered how it would affect Pete.

"Her going will not change the goals that Jim and I have in the work. Marriage is a long way off for them."

I wasn't too sure. I even wondered if Betty's decision to go had subtly led Pete to think about mending his relationship with me.

Somehow I survived that first awkward meeting with Pete since the breakup. I saw him only occasionally afterward. He had told me he would be leaving Seattle around the first of the year. He and Jim would spend a couple of weeks in Los Angeles visiting churches, and then they would board the boat for South America the first week of February. Pete spent his days buying and packing for Ecuador, and traveling out of town to speak. We had no opportunity to work at restoring our relationship, but it probably was just as well. I found it difficult to be with him; my emotions were too close to the surface. I

---

*A Brethren missions magazine, no longer published.

wanted him to tell me he loved me, or at least try to include me in his plans, but he didn't. Deep down, though, a part of me knew he was right in his decision: I was so young and still had university to finish. Pete might eventually learn to manage, but I knew I'd never survive down there. And his comments about Betty's gifts only made me realize how little I had to offer right now.

By Christmas our relationship had improved to a rather unemotional, but nevertheless pleasant, friendship. When Pete returned from a speaking appointment in Vancouver, he stopped by just before Christmas and, to my utter surprise, handed me a small box. The last thing I ever expected was a Christmas gift. I didn't buy anything for him.

It was a blue zircon ring.

"Pete, this is lovely. Why are you giving me this?"

"I saw it in Vancouver and I wanted it for you. Maybe you would think of me when you wear it."

"But why a ring?" I said, confused. To me a ring was symbolic if given by a man. What did Pete have in mind? I had hardly seen him in the last five months, and little had changed since he came back from New Jersey.

"I couldn't leave without letting you know that I still care for you," he said. "I still cannot give you any assurance about the future, and certainly not about marriage. But I thought this ring could symbolize my care and our friendship. There are no strings attached. I want you to be free to date. And I must also be free to apply myself totally to the work that's ahead of me. I can't be under pressure to write to you, and I guess mail service in the jungle is pretty infrequent."

"But what do I tell people about our situation?" I asked. "A ring could be misunderstood as an engagement." I knew I wasn't ready for an engagement, not now. He hadn't told me he loved me since that fateful Sunday in July. I couldn't assure him of my love now.

"It's not an engagement," he said firmly. "We could call it an 'understanding' between us. We know that we care for each other but do not know what God has for us in the future. If we let our emotions become involved we would be useless. I can't be burdened with that."

"That still means five or more years of uncertainty, Pete. How can we continue to put our emotions on hold?" Apparently he could do such a thing, but I couldn't.

"I don't know if it will be that long. I have to wait until I get there and see for myself what the needs are. I just don't know what the future is for the two of us there. I do know that I care for you and trust God to guide."

Even though it symbolized an "understanding" totally devoid of emotion, the ring did give me some hope for the future. It almost felt like a new beginning for us. For the first time I told Pete I was thinking of taking a few Spanish courses, and possibly accounting, with Ecuador in mind; he thought it was a great idea.

I spent the next few days looking for something that Pete could remember me by. The men had almost no room to bring personal items; mostly they packed practical things for jungle living. When I heard that he needed a coat, I thought this was the answer. When he tried it on, he said he really liked it, and he looked great. (It was the first time I had ever seen him in a decent topcoat.) I felt good. I had given him a useful, yet meaningful gift, one that would remind him of me. It seemed to mean a lot to him, too.

When the time finally came for him to leave Seattle, I couldn't watch. I cried through most of his church farewell and stayed in the background. He did kiss me good-bye as he left, however.

When Pete first broke our commitment, no one except our families and closest friends noticed. But as he left for Ecuador, people began to wonder what was going on. Some thought we had gotten engaged. It was hard to explain our "understanding." If it wasn't an engagement, what was it? people would say. My mother found it difficult to be asked about Pete and me, because she had seen all the emotional turmoil Pete had put me through. And the very thought of their only child going to Ecuador alarmed both of my parents.

David Dye, the one friend who knew us best, later gave his impression of our situation:

> Pete had left a girl behind in Seattle, Olive Ainslie, whom he loved very much. But he did not feel at that time that God would have him take Olive to the rugged pioneering ministry in Ecuador which he would be undertaking. While marriage is the norm for most people, it is not an inalienable right of the consistent Christian. Instead, God's will is first consideration. One who has not left a loved one far away may have difficulty appreciating the quality of trust that caused Pete to go, joyful in the Lord.[4]

Maybe Dave knew more than I did about Pete's feelings for me; maybe he knew less. But while he and others admired Pete for nobly sacrificing everything to follow God's will, I was left to pick up the pieces of my life—emotionally and spiritually.

Case in point: A few weeks after he had left Seattle, Pete gave away the beautiful coat I had bought him. "I saw my good friend here in Portland," he mentioned casually in a letter, "and he needed a coat more than I did, so I gave him the coat. I am sure you will understand."

I didn't. His generosity to someone else was a slap in the face to me—just one more indication that he didn't really care. Again he had hurt me. Maybe I had attached too much significance to the coat, I thought. But at one time he wouldn't have parted with *anything* I had given him. Now he was gone and he had nothing from me. I asked myself, Is this how a person is supposed to express his total commitment to do God's will? Where was the Pete I used to know—the one who had been totally committed to God, but had also been sensitive and warm and loving?

By the time Pete and Jim were to sail out of Los Angeles in February 1952, I had managed to let go of most of my anger over the coat. Pete even called me to say good-bye, and we had a generally upbeat conversation.

"Olive, I just met Ed and Marilou McCully—the other couple who will follow us out next year. He's finishing up his missionary medicine course at Biola."

"Oh yeah—the McCullys. My folks told me about them after visiting Ed's parents last October. I didn't realize he was at Biola, but I knew he and his wife were going to Ecuador. We've known his parents for a long time. You know, I used to have a picture of Ed and his brother from when they were in high school. Small world."

"Maybe you should write those two and ask Ed about the missionary medicine course," Pete suggested. "You might want to take it in the future. They are a wonderful couple. I think you would work well together. By the way, Jim thought it was great that you're taking accounting. It might come in handy on the field."

"Pete, you are talking as if you think I may be going down there."

"Who knows, Little One? I want you to know that I really care for you and trust that God someday will bring us together. That is all I can say for now. Hey, I bought you something with Marilou's help. Let me know how you like it when it arrives."

I dissolved into tears. Good-byes had always been hard, but this one tore me apart. I began to believe that he really did care. The future wasn't any clearer, but my hope had somehow been rekindled.

I did not hear Pete's voice again for two-and-a-half years.

A package from him arrived the week after he left. It was a very full, beautiful skirt of a patchwork pattern with tones of green and yellow. I loved it.

Before leaving Seattle, Pete had encouraged me to write to Betty Howard, who would be leaving for Ecuador herself in a few months, and I did. Her response, which came soon after the men arrived in Ecuador, was most significant to me because it further restored my hope that Pete loved me. She had come to know Pete while they were at Franconia Notch in New Hampshire, she wrote. "I had heard quite a bit about you . . . although I'm sure Pete disciplined himself to exercise as much taciturnity on the subject as he did!" I was surprised that Pete had spoken to Betty about me, since our relationship was totally in ruins at the time. Obviously, he had not told her the whole story. She continued:

> Pete read poetry to us. I can never forget it. He has a soul for poetry—for all literature—and this I appreciate especially. May God direct this propensity for His own glory always. There is always the possibility of a snare in any talent or ability, but the Lord speaks of the *transformation of the mind,* and loving Him "with all thy mind."

She went on to ask about my present plans:

> [I] am wondering if you intend to graduate at the U. or not. If not, is there any possibility of your going to Ecuador? I often think of you, and pray for you, Olive, knowing that if *my* very being is torn by Jim's going so far away, what must it be for you? For at least I am on my way there, whether or not I see him for years to come.

Her question about Ecuador encouraged me more than anything Pete had said, though I knew that if I did go, it wouldn't be any time soon.

Betty's words touched on several important areas to me. She quoted the verse, "If any man loves me, he will keep my word" (John 14:23), and then commented, "If this business of obedience at any cost does not involve the very pith and marrow of our being—yes, the most precious ties on earth, then it is not obedience, is it? But oh, what a blessed hope we have—an eternal weight of glory." As a teenager, I had read a book about knowing God's will. The author maintained that we would know his will if we obeyed him. So at that time I prayed that God would help me to know him. As I read Betty's letter, I began to wonder: Was the Lord taking me at my word and asking me to obey? What would obedience to God cost me?

Betty's next lines bewildered me, because I had not known how serious her relationship with Jim was:

When first I knew that I loved Jim, it called forth almost a feeling of resentment that God should have allowed the experience of loving (I knew it was the *one* experience which would cost *everything*) to come into my life. But I have nothing but praise now—over 3 1/2 years later. . . . I am glad—very glad, that Pete and Jim are together. They need one another, and are perfect complements, I believe. I am also glad that Pete has *you*. God saw that it was good. Ours is a solemn responsibility—just how solemn, we probably do not realize. . . . True in our love, through all the suffering that is forever the companion of loving. True through the bitterness of realization that a man's love *never* has the quality of constancy that we hope for. True in the willingness to sacrifice—for sacrifice is a woman's part. True in holding a man to the highest, when it would be so much easier to give way—for he looks for the highest, at the same time trying to persuade otherwise, but is disappointed if he does not find the highest.

I understood what she meant about suffering, because once I had declared my love for Pete there had been nothing but suffering. But was she saying this was to be expected? Did Pete really love me, but not in the way I had thought? Could I no longer expect him to be the same toward me now that God had called him? Her words made love seem so difficult and, for normal people like me, unattainable. It all sounded so spiritual, so unreal. What I think really happened between Pete and me, between all of us, is that we played hide-and-seek with our true feelings for each other. Unsure of the other's feelings, and unable (or unwilling) to express our own, we opted to relate on what seemed to be a higher, spiritual plane. Some of it undoubtedly came from the Spirit's prompting, but much of it masked real feelings of love, passion, doubt, fear, and indecision.

Betty also introduced me to the writings of Amy Carmichael in that letter. She included a quote from *His Thoughts Said . . . His Father Said:*

His thoughts were full of unspoken longing. His father said, Art thou here for the joy of being together? Thou hast eternity. The son answered, I know that I have eternity, but—His Father said, Is it too hard for thee to sell all that thou hast—even this—that thou mayest have treasure in heaven? The son asked to be shown what was meant by treasure in heaven. He was shown that it means the greater glory of his Lord, more jewels for His crown, and eternal overweight of joy because of the sword-cut which had set him free to serve without distraction. It meant the holy intimacy fore-shadowed by the words not yet fully understood. These are they which follow the Lamb whithersoever He goeth.[5]

Betty Howard had a good friend, Betty Paeth, who was a missionary candidate to the Philippines. Pete mentioned to me that Betty Paeth was attending the University of Washington for a year before going on to the Biola School of Missionary Medicine (where Ed McCully was studying), and suggested that I introduce myself. We liked each other immediately. During Pete's first few months in Ecuador, she and I spent much time together. She knew Betty Howard, Jim, and Bill Cathers very well, and became my main channel of information and insight about them all. Her perceptive understanding of Jim and Betty—and of their driving motivations—helped me considerably in those days of uncertainty. God had brought her into my life at just the right time.

9
MACHO
MISSIONARIES

*O*n the ship to Ecuador, Pete and Jim, excited to be underway at last, tried to prepare themselves for the new life of service to God that lay ahead. They talked, studied Spanish, reminisced, and planned their strategy for reaching people who had never heard the name of Jesus. Pete's diary entries and letters, as well as Jim's journal, reveal some of their thoughts and experiences during those days. Pete captured his feeling while standing out on the freighter's deck:

> A warm wind is whipping the sea into a frothy leaping, and glues your clothes to you in front and flaps them behind you. Thought of "The voice of Jehovah upon the water"—the surging power and grandeur and bigness of the wind upon the water; a human voice is puny and lost in the vacant howling of it.

At their second port of call in Central America, he wrote:

> It was *muy interesante;* adobe houses with thatched roofs, dozens of children in clothing "not much before, and rather less than half of that behind," dogs and pigs galore,

wired windows open because of the heat, two blaring public address systems, a "palatial" Hotel Miramar, some battered statues to lend a little culture, plenty of dust and drunk men.

One evening, as they sat on the deck singing and watching the "various color moods of a dying day," they discussed

girls we had gone with and the deliverance from wrong steps which we easily might have taken. Talked also of the promise of God to make us men, big men, quiet, mature, balanced, full of faith. To rest in that God knows what is good for us and will perform it for us rests our fretting minds as we feel not always coherent desires in ourselves to be men other than most of those whom we see; we have faith that God knows which of these inchoate longings are really for our best and those He will do for us. "Do Thou for me, Lord God, Do Thou."

Jim wrote of that night as well:

Pete and I talked long last night, mostly about women— Jeanine, Betty and Cammie and Olive. Joy in praying afterward. Pete gave me this from Teasdale:

"Let it be Forgotten"

Let it be forgotten
As a flower is forgotten,
A flower, and a fire
That once was singing gold.
Let it be forgotten
Forever and forever
Time is a kind friend
And he will make us old.[1]

Having been delivered from women, and their pasts forgotten, Pete and Jim appeared to be ready for the future.

On one of their stopovers, they tasted a world slightly less idealistic. A young woman got their attention, and as they struggled to converse in the little Spanish they knew, they realized that she was a young prostitute looking for clients.

> The directness and freshness of her and her approach shocked us; oh, the tragedy of her life, especially when she becomes old and others have the physical attraction. . . . Emilia stands now for us both as a burning and tragic symbol; a symbol of life sacrificed for lust. Oh, to be able to speak to such as her and give her living water. . . . The frustration in her face as it dawned upon her that we didn't want what she could give us. And her pert *adios* and the sight of her walking away with her head held high and her stride firm and measured won't be forgotten.

The physical and spiritual needs, everywhere so great, intensified their desire to bring the message of salvation to these people. In one town, Buenaventura, Colombia (called a "hole" by the ship's officers), Pete wondered what Jesus would have done amid such poverty and hostility.

> The fish and meat markets [were] worst of all; the meat . . . rotting was lying open on the bamboo poles, covered with flies, the stench was heavy and sickening and the floor was puddled with greenish-gray slime. . . . I did not feel sick, thank God, but was stunned by the impact it made—I wanted to withdraw and wizen up. . . . The town . . . rusted tin roofs and hot, dark, falling buildings follow each other monotonously, each presenting awful squalor. . . . only cries for "money" from children who followed us gave any signs of friendliness and it was put on with design. . . . I know [Jesus Christ] would be with

90

the people in the marketplace, but I wonder what He would do about the sanitation problems—would He work at it directly or indirectly?

This was Pete's first encounter with the poor of South America. He and Jim were told about an evangelical missionary from the United States who had served in this town. According to the story, he was

a swell fellow who fitted in well and who drove a truck to meet expenses. But the fellow had come down with a double fever, malaria and typhoid, which continued for seventeen days until finally they had taken him to Cali. There he arrived on Sunday and was not admitted to a hospital, only receiving a shot or two to hold him over till Monday. But sometime during the night he had taken a bread knife and slashed his throat right thru to the backbone. He left a wife and two small children, and the evangelical work here. To us the story was stark and shocking, and we felt no condemnation for the fellow. No doubt the fever had taken his sanity. But still the facts are shocking—and a warning. It could happen to us, to me. Oh God preserve. . . .

The gruesome story did not dampen their excitement, however, as they prepared to arrive in Ecuador the next day. Pete wrote:

I cannot summon any great emotion. In one sense tomorrow is only tomorrow. And yet to see it in the dimensions of our whole lives makes it a day of significance: it ends one life and begins another. Oh may it make us like Christ, and increase our *faith;* faith to expect miracles, in conversion, in discipline to discipleship, in establishing assemblies, in entering into our inheritance. I feel that the experiences I shall have will put the promises of God to the ultimate test, that this is a proving ground for God Himself, that God wants to justify Himself before our eyes by bringing to pass His word. And He will have to. We are going to the most discouraging and unlikely of situations—it is a test of God Himself as well as us. Our responsibility is to believe and to work, and expect God to vindicate His name by displaying His power. He has got to do it or it can't be done.

Then Pete quoted a few lines from the now-famous hymn:

We rest in Thee our Shield and our Defender
We go not forth alone against the foe
Strong in Thy Strength, safe in Thy keeping tender
We rest in Thee, and in Thy name we go. . . .

As they waited to go up the river to the port city of Guayaquil, Pete wrote: "I am a little excited for the first time, am fidgety, and find that time drags." During the potentially troublesome (and often costly) customs procedures, they read from the Psalms: "Oh God, forsake me not; until I have shewed thy strength unto this generation" (71:18 KJV). "Through God we shall do valiantly: for he it is that shall tread down our enemies" (60:12 KJV). They praised God after watching all their hand baggage go through customs with no charge. In their enthusiasm, they didn't even care that no one from the mission station met them at the dock.

Their first night in Ecuador gave them a foretaste of life in the jungles. Pete and Jim slowly realized that the "enemies" they sought God's protection from were not the kind they had anticipated. That evening they checked into a local hotel, desperately counting on a good night's sleep. "We were optimists," Pete wrote. "It was hot and humid; we were next door to a theater and our beds had occupants—so our first night in Ecuador was fitful and Jim got very little sleep as he waged an active war against mosquitoes and fleas, without notable success." Thus began their new life, different from anything they had known.

Well, almost anything. While staying in a missionary home in Guayaquil, waiting for all their barrels of supplies to clear customs, Pete wrote:

> Life on a mission station has many similarities to home life: dishes to be washed, beds made, babies to be bathed and cared for, cookies to be baked, etc., Sunday school lessons to prepare, flannelgraph to cut out, English spoken at tables. The well-known duties of life being the same anywhere is being impressed upon me. Unless faith empowers the small tasks life is the same, full of the humdrum and the menial.

Later, in Quito he wrote that life in a missionary home "could be construed as outside missionary sacrificial living: we have one full-time maid (12 hours a day), one part-time, full dinners where we all wear shirts and ties. . . ." But in contrast to the apparent affluence, there was "no central heating (it is cold in the mountain cities), cooking over three Coleman stoves, crowded conditions, all water boiled, food moderate and not too plentiful." (Of course, even these conditions were affluent compared to that of many local residents.)

Whatever Pete had envisioned about missionary life in this new country, he would quickly learn that ministry on the mission field was the same as ministry anywhere—a huge, difficult task that yielded some successes, some misunderstandings, and some failures. Pete described one missionary's pessimistic view of the evangelical church's strength in Ecuador:

> There are over one hundred missionaries in this small country, and some of the work has been going on for fifty

years and yet he does not think that the church could withstand wholesale persecution here as it did in Colombia. . . . Bible school graduates are not doing well, are easily offended, are proud of their position thinking that the receiving of a diploma makes them somebody, and that being ordained and allowed to wear a black suit and special black tie elevated them above ordinary believers. Some graduates have left the ministry . . . [some] have been released from the school . . . because of immorality.

Other graduates were "too young to be fully received by older congregations, and also are not fully supported by their congregation." (The national church at that time depended on foreign funds for most of its support.)

"All these facts raise so many questions in my mind as to missionary principles," Pete concluded,

and right now my premature judgment is that we have taken over most of the forms of American fundamentalism and invariably thought that Latin American Christianity should take similar or identical forms, and have forced many of them to be adapted when they do not adequately fit this area (let alone the problem deeper still, as to whether these forms are Biblical at all)! To me there is real tragedy here!!!

Later Pete found more cause for concern: Of the various ministries in Ecuador involving missionaries, very few were directly engaged in church planting.

Another "enemy" Pete faced in his early days there was language study. It required all his effort and concentration. In spite of his intelligence and disciplined study habits, he soon knew he was not mastering Spanish quickly enough. After a month in a missionary home in Quito, where only English was spoken, he realized he needed to be in the home of a national.

He had to be immersed in Spanish if he was to learn it fast, "because we fear that if we don't get Spanish now, and get it correctly and with proper accent we never shall."

Although both Pete and Jim wanted less contact with English-speakers, they were not able to find a room in an Ecuadorian home for two more months. In the meantime, Pete's difficulty in learning the language weighed heavily on him. He called language study "a tyranny of frustration and I expect much more of myself than I can produce and I am continually impatient with myself for not learning more and not being able to say it better." At times he felt overwhelmingly useless, but he also believed that if he gave himself over to study, God would give him the language.

> I want to hit Spanish harder than ever now and at times hate the frequency of English contact. Oh well, I must be content as we only arrived in Ecuador two months ago today. I don't cease to praise God that I am here—freed from a life which could have been so brittle, and bookish and dull, and pushed out to the frontier. Hallelujah!

Another unexpected "enemy" the men encountered was a heavy social calendar. Other missionaries often invited them out to dinners and gatherings attended only by fellow missionaries. Pete and Jim enjoyed the fellowship, but also felt pulled away from their ministry and from the Spanish-speaking people. "It is good," Pete summed up,

> but it is not the sort of thing I came to Ecuador for; life at home was too full of it. And it is increasingly obvious that a missionary could spend practically all his time in this type of nicety. I trust God preserves me from it. I want to get to needy people and train disciples, and see Indians come into the kingdom. The closer I get to the Oriente [eastern jungles], the more intense my interest in Indians

and I have felt in the last couple days great prayer longing for them, in particular the Aucas (after reading T's notes on them). It is the first really deep desire I have felt for them and I do want to be burdened, committed to the work there "laying down my life for their faith." Only this type of prayer burden and life committal does God honor, I believe, with real blessing.

In less than three months in Quito, Pete had experienced the problems of the missionary, the needs of the work, the discouragement of language study, and the frustration of not being able to communicate to the nationals. Though he struggled, he did not lose heart.

He kept his family up to date with fascinating, descriptive letters. I was thankful to receive carbon copies. I marveled at his powers of observation and his ability to write with such detail. Though I looked forward to these letters, they weren't written to me personally and gave me little encouragement about our relationship. He usually scrawled a note to me at the bottom of each letter but never indicated he was lonely or that he missed me. Maybe he was being guarded because he did not want to raise my hopes, I thought, or perhaps he didn't have time to think about "us" because of his heavy study load. I still yearned for some words of assurance about our future.

I later discovered that he was recording his own thoughts and struggles with loneliness in his diary. Had I known the content of these and other diary entries about me, I'm sure many of my doubts about Pete would have been quelled. Unfortunately, it would be some time before I knew with certainty how he felt. For example, during a particularly discouraging time with his language study he wrote,

It is just in such a "lost" and depressed situation that a wife is a great encouragement. . . . her approving love and evaluation of you, based as it is on what you are (as she sees it) is a comfort and stability to you now in your present state when your evaluations of yourself are based only on the immediate. In a more remote way, Olive's love for me encourages me. I'm glad, genuinely glad, to know she loves me even though she cannot be here to demonstrate it. The remembrance of it even helps, and interjects another perspective, a more encouraging one into the present view of myself. It assists in keeping me from dejection.

A month later he wrote in his diary:

> How I love Olive today. She has been on my mind most of the day, and I feel most drawn to her. I am so glad she is so quiet and shy, so beautifully shy, and not forceful and loud—the more I know myself the more confident I am that God has led us together and fitted us for each other, giving us blending personalities. I rejoice to see the way she is going ahead spiritually on her own—for example, her going last weekend to the Nav conference by herself. It is of the Lord. Knowing that she is pressing ahead and knowing that she loves me gives me such stability in my thinking and centralizes and purifies my desire. The faithfulness of her love calls forth faithfulness from me, and does its part to make me content to wait God's time.

At the end of their second month in Quito, Betty Howard joined them. When Pete first heard that she was coming he wrote, "Her being here will form some psychological and emotional problems for Jim, which will be real but intangible— God knows." Upon her arrival, he wrote: "She looked strikingly tall and attractive in a dark blue suit and hat, a filmy blouse beautifully made, red shoes and a bright red coat carried on her arm. . . . I feel for her and Jim: the pull must be strong."

Shortly thereafter I received a long, single-spaced, typed

letter from Pete—not a family form letter, but a personal one. First came all the news and prayer requests. Then he wrote of Betty and Jim.

It is not easy for them especially as there can be no overt signs of real interest in each other, but simply the pose of being missionary colleagues. Jim says that emotionally their situation is "una lucha" [a struggle] to maintain and keep. . . . They are thinking about engagement within a year to make the problem a little easier but nothing is settled about that.

At the end of Pete's letter, I found, for the first time since he had gone to Ecuador, some lines of encouragement:

Don't be discouraged about your Spanish—at least get a good reading knowledge. . . . Use it constantly until you get here. Must close now "little one" but not without assuring you of my constant love and devotion. We are happy now and God is going to bring us to real happiness together in His time. These are days for deepening the spiritual lives within us in order to draw us to the Lord and each other. I want no one else but you, so be encouraged and rejoice.

I should have been ecstatic at seeing this first assurance of his love since our breakup. Instead, I tried to second-guess his motives. He was only feeling this way because Betty had just arrived, I told myself. Besides, it bothered me that Pete seemed more concerned about Jim and Betty's hard time—heightened by her presence—than he was with *our* uncertain future. He kept saying that our difficult days would deepen our spiritual lives. But what about love and companionship and desire? Was it too much to expect him to want these things as well?

10
SEARCH FOR
GUIDANCE

*W*hile I worried about God's will for my relationship with Pete, Pete and Jim were striving to understand His will for the work in Ecuador. The first step, they decided, would be to reopen the station at Shandia in the eastern jungles and reestablish the ministry among the Quichua Indians. Once Shandia was operational, Pete and Jim hoped that the Cathers would take their place, freeing the two single men to begin a ministry in some other Quichua village. Ultimately they dreamed of a future outreach to the Cofanis and the Aucas. Pete wrote in his diary:

> We long to reach these as yet untouched. I long to see the jungles as proving ground for divine Biblical operation— as a place for us to put into action Biblical principles for missionary work, and watch God act in response to them and to our faith for His work (*God give me faith!!!*). The jungles are relatively untouched and I would love to see God use them as a large-scale "experiment" and demonstration to us, to spirit worlds, etc. of what can be done to immoral, shifty, treacherous people when they are con-

fronted with Pauline missionary action (as God gives us to see it).

No doubt Dr. Tidmarsh's desire to reopen Shandia and continue the work among the jungle Indians was driving both Jim and Pete. But they also sensed the need for divine guidance as they planned their strategy. After Pete heard more about Dr. Tidmarsh's experience, he reflected on how tricky it can be to determine God's will:

Tidmarsh told me an interesting bit of his own life which is a good example of complexities in guidance. After he and Gwen were driven out of Loreto they wondered whether his jungle work might be over. After recuperating in Quito they thought they might be being led toward one of the southern Sierra cities, and felt that if they could find a suitable house to live in and hold meetings in this would be an indication of the Lord's will. They found a questionably suitable house which Gwen thought was the house, but T. didn't. Anyway, T. put down money on it to hold it while they prayed about it and then left to finish up his affairs in the jungles. While there he received word that the owner of the house had backed out on the deal and rented it to another party. And at the same time seeing the possibility of work in Shandia felt he ought to go back to jungle work. Gwen didn't. Still he went back and opened up Shandia and the indirect result was Gwen's accident and the termination of jungle work for both of them.

In contrast to Dr. Tidmarsh, Pete and Jim felt they knew clearly where God wanted them. And they assumed that the two couples, the Cathers and the McCullys, felt the same way. But in the second month after their arrival in Ecuador, they learned they had assumed too much. Bill Cathers told Pete and

Jim that he thought God was leading him in a different direction. He felt drawn to work with the Colorado Indians, a primitive jungle tribe in the western Andes. He was seriously thinking about temporarily overseeing the Spanish ministry in San Miguel and Santo Domingo, two small towns near that tribe. He and Irene would fill in for Dee and Marie Short, a Brethren missionary couple going back to the States on furlough, and perhaps begin a new outreach to the Colorados when the Shorts returned. Pete summed up Bill's concerns about going to Shandia:

> He is afraid that if he took over Shandia (1) it would involve his being tied down there for a long time and he feels that he would like to be freer than this would involve, particularly if the school is begun, (2) he feels an open clash with T. is almost inevitable. (3) He senses [that] T. views Shandia as *his* work on *his* land with *his* Indians and in *his* house and that his hands would be tied there (in this I think he is not quite right). Thus the work among the Colorados, an untouched people in a pioneering situation, appeals to him as it seems more what he feels called to and with fewer chances for sidetrack. I feel B. ought to go *very slow* and visit both Miguel and Shandia before he makes up his mind before God.

Bill's inclinations appeared to stem as much from his reluctance to work with Dr. Tidmarsh as from his sense of divine guidance. Maybe he thought he was heeding the apostle Paul's principle of not building on another man's foundation (Romans 15:20). However, Pete followed this comment on Bill's announcement with some personal insights:

> [Bill] is not at all accustomed to the abruptness, the propriety, the distance, the directorship, the aristocratic tendencies of Dr. Tidmarsh. I sympathize with him

because he is just being introduced to the British way of life in its aristocratic form and he chafes under it, and inwardly rebels. It forms almost no problem for me because I have known it, even though not admired it, all my life. T. acts very similarly to Dad, especially in disciplinary matters and in his "picayunishness." I love him though—he is a paradox of breadth and narrowness. Fortunately his narrowness only seems to be in small habits and idiosyncrasies, and his largeness embraces most basic principles of spiritual life and missionary procedure. I am glad we are with him.

This entry showed Pete's awareness of the human factor in relations between missionaries and how it bears on issues of guidance. He also showed that spirit of acceptance I admired in him.

While on a survey trip down to San Miguel, Pete wrote further about the problem of guidance:

Bill has decided to relieve Dee and Marie Short for furlough which would delay his coming to Shandia by a year and a half at least. I don't like it, but if we walk in faith that God alone is going to guide us, then I take this by faith too and say nothing. God must be sovereign.

Since Bill's announcement had raised a number of questions, the Brethren missionaries all met together in Quito for a day to discuss the future of their work in both the western and eastern jungles. They talked openly about whether Bill and Irene should go to San Miguel and Santo Domingo. Pete was afraid that once the Cathers went to the western jungles, they would probably never go to Shandia. He also felt that the Cathers, who had only studied Spanish for two months, needed more time before taking on the Shorts' responsibilities. Bill felt it was a "necessity" to relieve them.

Pete wrote philosophically about Bill's approach to discerning God's will:

> I am doubtful about the *necessity* of relieving them though I think it a very good thing. The necessity is not *objective* in terms of either Biblical or missionary principles, but is *subjective* in the minds of Bill & Irene in that they feel the call of God. They go, it seems to me, (if they go) not because the work demands it, but only because God directs them—this latter is the sovereign necessity.

The open discussion proved to be constructive, and brought hope for more times of prayer and counseling together. Soon afterward there was news from Bill. Pete wrote:

> Bill said this afternoon that though he has felt a strong burden for the Colorados he has not sensed any call there and that he is still planning to join us at Shandia after . . . Santo Domingo, God willing. Praise be! I hope he comes for our hearts are knit and he feels as we do about the principles of operation in carrying out God's work.

Bill had decided to relieve the Shorts, but rather than pursue further outreach to the Colorados afterward, he and Irene would go to Shandia.

(Although the Cathers fully intended to join Pete and Jim in Shandia, they never did. Various circumstances later forced them to return to the States. After the five men were killed, they eventually went back to Ecuador and worked in Shandia.)

Experiences such as this on the field caused everyone to think more deeply about how to discern God's will and his "call." Pete wrote, "This afternoon Betty and I had a good talk about guidance and the 'PBI' [Prairie Bible Institute] approach to spirituality." He then compared his ideas to those attributed to that school. Stating that "basically the problem is faith," he proceeded first to explain his own position:

When I at the beginning of the day place myself in God's hands and ask for guidance it is a matter of faith that I receive it. I am in the will of God and I have the Spirit to guide me in praise and thanksgiving as I walk that day and should I confront situations of temptation it is the ministry of the Spirit to alert me and direct me; and if I fall confession restores me. God's will and its problems are simplified for me then; I am in the will of God whether I missed my bus, got caught in a rainstorm, left my textbook home, suffer from dispepsia, etc.

Then he described the "PBI conception of spirituality," which

sees me not so much as in the will of God now, but beginning with *nothing* and starting to claim things—the person is not an entity led now in this moment by God Himself but a vacuum and a bad-smelling one at that—or a vessel which ought to be a vacuum and needs to be emptied of self in order to be filled with the Spirit.

"It is so close to the truth that it is hard to criticize helpfully," he continued,

but again I think the crux is faith: faith to believe that God has forgiven; faith to rest in all the vicissitudes of life that God is guiding; faith to praise when things don't *look* like the will of God or that God is guiding; faith to praise in all circumstances; faith to see that the flesh now has died already and that my privilege is to be "alive unto God." Thank God for the liberty of the position—it allows a man to be a man, allows him joyfully to live in the life (circumstances) that he *must* live in; it places spirituality in reach. I am not forever in Romans 7 trying to get into Romans 8; I am right now "alive unto God," in the will of God, aware that the Spirit fights for me against the flesh (often without my being conscious of all aspects of the struggle) and I am ready to praise and to intercede. Thank God I am not a slave any more to an unrealistic and unbiblical spiritual ideal; I am alive now to live to God's glory, to center my life and thinking around Christ, to *walk* in the Spirit now. Amen. My Spirit, rise up and bless God!

The missionaries clearly held diverse views of guidance. Dr. and Mrs. Tidmarsh had disagreed over where to conduct their ministry, but then found both opinions vetoed by a plane crash. Jim seemed to be resigned to a tension between his idealism about singleness and his love for Betty, and still looked for a "sign" that he should marry her. To Betty, who was more intuitive about God's will, self-sacrifice figured prominently. Bill took into account the varying levels of need among the tribes, and the human dimensions of missionary teamwork. Pete believed he could trust in God's overruling even when humans misinterpreted His will.

11
ATTITUDES

"*El hijo del hombre no vino para ser sevide sino para servir.*" ("The Son of Man came not to be served, but to serve," Matthew 20:28.)

During those first months in Quito, Pete's diary entries showed how he learned to identify and confront the problems of ministry in another culture.

He and Jim often took Christian nationals on hikes, which were excellent opportunities to practice Spanish. They would learn all they could from the young men about the language and culture, and also encourage them in their faith. On one of these hikes, a national believer talked about his observations of methods used by the various missions. His words must have impressed Pete, for he noted that the man had "become alert to the issues of salary for national workers, freedom to move where God and not a mission directs, the danger of being servants of men and pleasers of them, the treachery of viewing the Lord's service as a job."

Pete then examined his own motives as a missionary:

God is not trying to train leaders but servants, and for the Oriente he is not going to equip Jim and me as jungle-wise leaders, but as humble servants for poor Indians. Nothing is so diametrically opposed to my natural desires which transfer without difficulty into the spiritual world the desires for attention to be thought spiritual and wise in the Scriptures, to direct spiritual work, to be recognized for work accomplished. I have got to be trained as a slave, committed to my brothers without reserve; not caring who does the work or who gets the credit for it, but only that God does it and gets praise from it. Like Christ who, when he received all things of the Father, took the disciples' feet in his hands and washed them. Oh God, to be satisfied with foot washing. Even the desire to excel in language study is tricky because it is so closely linked with the desire to be recognized as a leader—and (instead of sharing interesting insights into Spanish idioms with the other missionaries, as a servant should) I often find myself hoarding them as though by their weight the balance to test intelligence would tip in my favor.

I am serious, O Humbler of Hearts, before thee is the desire to be servant of all, so help in the desire by highlighting attitudes that prohibit against the backdrop of this revolutionary teaching: the lower one goes the higher he reaches.

Like most missionaries, Pete struggled over how to develop friendships with nationals who were not believers. *How do missionaries get to know the nationals?* he wondered. They don't work with them, their children go to different schools, they often live in walled compounds, and they often have a radically different standard of living. As he packed all his possessions for the jungle, Pete felt keenly aware of the barriers between him and the people he longed to reach.

"Have been concerned . . . with having so much, while almost everybody in Ecuador has so little," he wrote.

I seem against my real desire to be outside of the footsteps of the "man who had nowhere for his head." It is not that our equipment is impractical or in excess (quite the opposite) but that everything I have as necessary is judged by other standards than are found here. The real problem arises from our coming from a rich country where we were just ordinary into a poor country where we are immediately viewed as well-off by their standards. And by their standards they are right—we are rich and since we come to their country we are bound by their estimations. The thing is: how to be Christlike when you are viewed as rich; yet to give away almost all the clothes and equipment which we brought here to equip a jungle station is difficult. . . . This is the problem, heightened by the observation that sometimes Jim and I appear to the Ecuadorians as "well-paid gringos on a soft job." . . . this judgment is very difficult to shake loose. . . . And it hinders our testimony for to them we appear as wealthy gringos preaching to poor hungry Ecuadorians without doing anything to help them. Even to have a car appears a sign of wealth and yet to reach outlying towns a car is necessary. It is a real problem.

At present only two possible answers come to mind: (1) We cannot identify Christ always as "materially poor;" what we follow in Him is not literal poverty for its own sake but a *spirit of poverty*. "Blessed are the poor in spirit."

(2) We ought to rid ourselves of as many unessentials as possible—keeping our life as simple and frugal as health and circumstances will allow. I think we need to rethink the whole problem of maids: it can and has been very harmful. . . . Dorothy tells me that some Christian maids can never get to church because they have to be in

the house cooking the dinner for the missionaries. . . . The maid is only the symbol of the larger problem of how to be all things to all men. About Shandia I am reserving judgment until I see the situation but I want always to be willing to change . . . if necessary and in the steps of the Master.

Once Pete and Jim moved into a Spanish-speaking home to learn the language, they had more opportunities to be in close contact with nationals. On one occasion Pete described a ride to the country in a pickup truck:

Jim and I had a most instructive time, going with a crowd from the neighborhood. . . . The trip, on the picturesque road which follows a deep narrow valley through the big hill to the east of Quito, was most enjoyable, and on the way back under a delicately curved crescent moon we sang ourselves hoarse in the cold night air on the few Ecuadorian songs that we knew. I get a feeling of goodness and rightness when we get away from all "gringo" contact and immerse ourselves in their life and way of doing things. The quinta [country farm] is almost now beyond repair, but still contains some valuable paintings, some architecturally interesting foundation stones of different construction and supposedly dating back to the Inca times and some unkept fruit trees back of the house. We drank "chicha" made from corn for the first time, and also ate "tostados" hot from the fire and drank hot cinnamon water (also for the first time).

We visited the old church there and saw two priceless items of the colonial days: a helmet and shield of pure pounded silver with floral designs beaten into them; in the long somber silence and dim flickering candle light from the altar with absurdly and crudely painted crucifixion scenes looking down at us from the cobwebbed shadows.

Worship is based on loftiness and unapproachableness and impersonality—the somberness [quiets] the spirit, the array of dimly lighted ornamentals gives the impression of something important but unknowable, and the cold dank atmosphere pushes the spirit away from even the desire for spiritual intimacy with the images presented. The element of holy mystery and forbidden territory and ingrained habits of worship (like kneeling at the altar but not approaching it) symbolize and in another sense produce the prominent feature of Latin American Christianity: the desire to follow afar off.

In another encounter with the locals at an Ecuadorian fiesta—to which it was a great privilege to be invited—an unexpected problem arose.

We had an experience Tuesday night which has raised the problem of liberty and stumbling very forcibly and complexly. Jim and I and Dorothy went to an Ecuadorian fiesta in honor of Don Enrique . . . without knowing what it would involve, but being urged by the Arias' [a Christian neighbor couple] to go for courtesy. When there we discovered it was a *typical* fiesta consisting mainly of dancing and drinking cocktails.

All of us at first drank a cocktail, not knowing for sure what it was and later drank a couple more while others danced (none of them more than a mouthful or two) and we tried in Spanish to explain why evangelicals didn't. To compensate for our not dancing we joined the spirit as much as possible, having rather a hilarious time and Dorothy even danced when practically forced into it. We left early and accompanied three senoritas, one rather tipsy, to the bus (a serious social error, as we should have taken them home), and discussed a little our actions to each other as we walked home; all agreed it was a rather difficult situation and we wondered if we had acted wisely and at the same time thinking that it was into just such situations that Christ went, though without defiling himself.

Yesterday came the reaction.

(1) Betty was upset all day over our actions, feeling them to be wrong and contrary to Biblical principles; also she thought that D. being a relatively new Christian had been stumbled by our liberty, and argued that D. would not have drunk any liquor if we hadn't (rather dubious since she took hers before we were offered ours). She cried and was moody all day over it.

(2) Dorothy was disturbed by Betty's reaction, and thought maybe we had stumbled Betty. She was completely unsettled and said she wanted to talk with me further; her thinking appeared to be running along these lines: the fiesta was not very different from a party of unsaved people in the States and that taking a drink here had the same connotation as taking a drink in the States.

(3) Jim still had complete liberty in doing what he did, though he didn't approve of D. dancing for he feels that there are Scriptural principles which prohibit that type of dancing while he feels that there are no such which directly apply to taking for courtesy several mouthfuls of liquor. Both he and I agree that we would not indulge if believers were there who might be stumbled by our action nor would we speak of our action to such.

(4) I still felt liberty, but also had gained the info that Ecuadorian evangelicals didn't go to this type of fiesta, regarding it as worldly, which knowledge might well affect a future decision if another invitation comes. I do not feel that even dancing of this type is wrong, per se, and don't judge Dorothy for dancing—nor do I person-

ally feel that the taste of liquor is sin. But there is one thing I would like to note carefully—the reaction of Enrique and Clara [the party's guest of honor and his wife] when we present the gospel to them after having seen us act thus; the question is: will it seem antithetical and inconsistent to them? Or would it make difficult future work by other evangelicals with them, who might not share our broad views of liberty. All I am asking God to do is to make the issues clear from this experience; to make it instructive by giving incontestable evidence for one viewpoint.

Pete was realizing that the missionaries' relationships could be strained by their differing opinions about lifestyle. He understood why Jim had from the start looked for friends to join him in Ecuador: It would be easier to work with people they knew well, and who shared the same view of Scripture in regard to ministry. Even with compatible co-workers, however, conflicts were bound to arise. Often tensions resulted merely from lack of communication, but sometimes they did not.

When Betty and Dorothy had arrived, dynamics had changed among the missionaries. Betty had paired off with Jim, leaving Dorothy alone, unless Pete asked her to walk with him. After one of those walks he wrote: "I knew she was lonely and troubled . . . lonely for companionship." She needed someone to share her feelings with, and had expected to confide in Betty. But now Betty had Jim.

But in that same conversation, Pete discovered Dorothy had another problem faced by many missionaries: finances.

On this she poured out her heart, almost crying, in the bewildered state of now experiencing what she (and I) thought God would never allow a child of his to pass through. Recently she had had to write a bad check to meet obligations here. . . . This is shocking, and I have no pat answer to a girl in distress with such a problem. Frankly, I did not expect that God would allow it but then He does not give us the option of choosing the types of testing. I feel I've got to give her some money; I wish I had been sensitive to God's voice earlier. It wrings my heart to see her like this, especially when I know nothing to say that doesn't sound trite, but God is undoubtedly disciplining and channeling her spirit; perhaps he is giving her one of the most difficult testings of all: the discipline of embarrassment, forced and inevitable.

Dorothy had been serving for only four months, and was already having financial problems. Like most Brethren missionaries, she had been sent out with no guarantee of support from her home assembly. The Brethren felt that missionaries were to go out on faith, trusting the Lord to supply their needs. Missionaries would gain visibility by speaking at various assemblies, sharing their vision (though not asking for money), and hoping that enough assemblies would provide financial support. Since women were not allowed to speak in an assembly meeting, however, a single missionary woman's task of making herself known became quite difficult. As Pete's diary indicated, he had no simple answer to her dilemma. Does God test those who desire to serve him in this way? Pete wasn't sure.

Thankfully, Pete had no financial troubles at that time, probably because he was a man and an excellent speaker. (Jim's friendship and electrifying presence didn't hurt either.)

That summer, Pete summed up his first six months in Ecuador with this upbeat diary entry:

Well, these days in Quito have been good; "there has not failed one word of all the good promise which He promised." These almost six months have been crammed full of goodness and God has given us special privileges by the way of having no set responsibilities, of giving us the

113

money and the freedom to live with a national family and undoubtedly we have learned things that will stand us in good stead all our missionary lives. And it has been a terrific boon to our missionary lives—living free, with sufficient funds, praying together and seeing God give us faith, getting more and more from the Spanish Bible, gradually finding Spanish easier and getting useful phrases fixed in my mind so I didn't have to think out every one.

It has all been good and we have learned things: how to live with other missionaries, how to keep our mouths shut on some subjects, how to get along with the nationals, what their perspective of missionaries is. Tonight the [Ecuadorian] family told me that now I was talking as much or even more than Jim (and that he was slipping!), and that I had excellent pronunciation—sure was encouraging even though I knew more than to believe it all. I think another six months here in an Ecuadorian home would about seal it, but it has not pleased God to give it to us, and I *believe* that we are not going to suffer as a result. God is going to give us Spanish by one means or another, and Quichua as well.

The Fleming family, 1940: Father, Pete, Mary, Ken, and Mother.

Above: Pete and Olive in Seattle in 1951.

Left: Peter Fleming in Ecuador in 1952 or 1953.

Left: Olive in the skirt Pete sent her from Los Angeles.
Right: Pete clearing Shandia to accommodate the airstrip and buildings, October 1952.

Pete with Quicha Indians at Shandia.

July 1953; one of the first houses to go over the cliff during the flood that destroyed Shandia.

Left: Pete and Olive, the wedding day, Seattle, June 26, 1954.

Right: The bridge that was washed out and the *tarabita* used to cross the river during Olive's first trip to the jungles.

Left: Pete and Olive in front of the house at Puyupungu.

Right: The Flemings, McCullys, and Elliots on Christmas Day 1955 in Arajuno. The last Christmas together.

Pete with "George" on the beach.

Above: The MAF plane stripped by the Aucas.

Left: Olive at Shell Mera after the men were killed.

Left: Olive with the president of Ecuador at the time the evangelical missions were honored.

Right: The last time that all five widows were together, January 1957.

Left: The Quito house Pete and Olive lived in when they first arrived in November 1954.

Right: On Olive's return in January 1989, she found the same road and site of their first house much changed.

Arriving at Toñampare, January 1989. *From left:* Dayuma, Rachel Saint, and Olive.

Daughter Holly with baby monkey, 1989.

In the Waorani church. *From left:* Komi, Kimo, Walter, Olive, Dayuma, and Dawa.

Going down the river to Palm Beach, 1989. Rachel Saint at the front.

Palm Beach

Kimo and Dawa with Walter and Olive on Palm Beach.

Walter

Olive

The family together today. *From left:* David and Robin Liefeld, Jonathan and Beverly Hancock, Holly, and Olive and Walter Liefeld.

12
ANTICIPATION

*I*n his letters home from Quito, Pete seldom referred to the Aucas. His diary entry on March 30, 1952, however, records a strategy discussion with Dr. Tidmarsh for reaching that tribe. They had just learned that two Auca women, one of whom was a teenager by the name of Dayuma, were working at a *hacienda* several hours from the Shandia station. Pete wrote:

> I am keyed up just now about work in the Oriente. T. mentioned an approach to the Aucas which is thrilling to me. It is a sort of three step plan: (1) Open up Shandia while learning Quichua and getting the know-how to handle Indians; (2) Move to Ila in order to evangelize the Quichua-speaking area, and talk to the Auca women who were captured and who are now living at Ila, learning as much of the language of Aucas as possible; and (3) move then to Huito which is just to the south of Auca territory and live there, evangelizing the nearby Quichua speakers and waiting opportunity to somehow reach the Aucas from this side. Sounds fascinating. I am longing now to reach the Aucas if God gives us the honor of proclaiming the Name among them.

At about the same time, Pete wrote me about an Auca vocabulary list that Dr. Tidmarsh got from the captured girl. Then he wrote:

Do pray about the [Auca] problem, because it is a terrific one, and we are not sure what God wants us to do about it. We feel God may be directing us to work with them ultimately, but of course we are still not saying anything definitely about it to anyone.

Then he told me that Jim and Betty were considering engagement. Even though it would ease their relationship and help others understand what was going on, Jim was not ready for that commitment. Pete's diary explains why.

I want above all not to stand in his way at all if he feels it's God's will to marry Betty whenever he may do so. The feeling hit him (Jim) today more strongly than before that we have stayed single in order to do that which *can't* be done by married folks, and that work among the Yumbos [Quichuas] isn't in this category (even Tidmarsh took Gwen to Loreto!). The outstanding work which looms in the mind is the Aucas (and also the possibility of the Cofanis—we won't know how accessible they are till we get more information). The Aucas have been on my mind, too, though the thought scares me at times. But I am ready and my face is turned toward them. We have believed God for miracles and this may include the Aucas; it has got to be by miracles in response to faith, and no lesser expedient is a short-cut. Oh God guide!

Jim expressed similar thoughts in his journal at this time. For him, the die had been cast the first time he had heard about the Aucas; for Pete, when he first heard about the Aucas from Jim. But when it came to love, Jim's constant wavering about engagement almost seemed like insincerity. I felt that Pete's inconsistency with me had resulted from Jim's influence.

Although I still had no clear assurance from Pete about our future together, I began to make some decisions about my own life. First, I decided to suspend my studies at UW at the end of the school year. My intended major, occupational therapy, would be useless if I were eventually to join Pete in jungle work. I wanted to apply to the missionary medicine program Ed McCully had just taken at Biola, but I had no money and no guarantee that I would be going to Ecuador.

My father suggested that I get a job and prove myself in the workplace before going to a foreign mission field. I thought about that possibility: A job would provide the necessary funds, put me into the work world, and give me another year to test God's leading. In late spring, I received a job offer. But after much prayer and heart searching, I decided to (in a way) put God to the test that summer. Instead of accepting the offer, I took a Civil Service exam with a fall job in mind. That way I could still pursue a summer ministry at Camp Imadene.

In July 1952, Pete took his first journey down the narrow road through the Pastaza River valley to Shell Mera, a small town on the jungle's edge. He described the trip as "misty, foggy but most impressive. . . . The walls of the valley are somber in mist—stark and unfriendly." In Shell Mera Jim and Pete met some of the missionaries with whom they would be working shortly. They also made "a survey flight of Arajuno and the headwaters of the Nushino and Curaray rivers looking for Auca houses but without success. It was my first view of our inheritance and it was big, big, big, and thrilling." At last he had laid eyes on the Auca territory. There was no turning back now.

But as Pete's desire to reach the Aucas grew, so did his struggle with his feelings toward me. I, of course, didn't know this, since he said nothing about either the Aucas or about me in his family newsletters. Pete knew if he mentioned his desire to go to the Aucas, he would upset his family. So he tended not to express his deepest feelings of joy or struggle or fear in his letters, reserving them instead for his diary. There he could also write what he felt about me without any fear of misunderstanding. He was too far away, and anticipated too many years apart, to make any serious commitment to me, but his comments about my letters showed that I was communicating my love in spite of my doubts about his. "I rejoice over her spiritual growth and thank God for her love," he wrote at one point. "It is a tremendous boost to me here and will be even more so, I guess, in the jungles."

Pete's diary entries for July reflect greater confidence and excitement as the first phase of their training in Quito was nearing its end. His Spanish came easier. He could participate more fully in the work and communicate with the people. For several weeks during the summer, he served at a Christian camp in Ecuador, counseling a group of boys. Although their Spanish posed a new challenge for his language skills ("Kids talk so fast and all at once and are very blunt"), he found great fulfillment in his ministry with them. "A swell bunch, especially those of my group . . . and I learned lots from them." (At least one of those "swell" boys later became a well-known Christian leader in Latin America: Rene Padilla.)

As the time drew near to leave for the jungles, his anticipation of reaching the Indians ran high: "We were really going," he marveled. "It's like climbing a peak with the *idea* of reaching the top dominating every step, and then suddenly raising the head above some rock or cornice and seeing the top itself in front of you—the idea becomes palpable."

I couldn't say I felt the same way. The closer the time came for him to leave, the more I feared for our relationship. Letters would be fewer. Phone calls were unheard of. In the days before he left Quito, however, he wrote several times to me privately about our relationship.

He recorded his feelings about one of the letters he sent in his diary:

> The freshness of love for Olive was very strong. . . . I wrote [to her] as frankly as I ever have, about our love and some thoughts about why God may have suspended it as it is: largely so that we may have a qualitative enjoyment of it in its position now without just viewing it as a step to greater intimacy. How God has given us sweetness and joy in our love—it does not cease to make me feel warm inside when I think of her and what God has given us and will yet give us.

I received these letters at Camp Imadene, and they calmed me somewhat. I must have responded frankly to him, since my letter prompted a long diary entry:

> She is so honest and pure and the openness of her love brings me out of the subtle, submerged and scheming consciousness which is me—"She will do me good and not evil all the days of her life." I wonder now how I could ever have thought of being without her in life (not that I question the guidance and testings of those days); she seems so right for me, so beautiful in her tenderness and frankness, so undesigning as she lives with the drive of her love for me, so tragic in the loneliness of going out from her cabin of girls and crying out on the point while all her little girls are sleeping, restful in the knowledge of her competence. Her modesty in describing her rescue of a drowning girl is so typical of the unspoiled freshness which is Olive, and such a contrast to the mental slavery of wringing dry every thought and possibility and the

restless washing machine-like churning of my mind. Oh, I love her tonight for being what I am not.

If only Pete had told me all that he wrote in his diary, I probably never would have doubted his love and devotion to me again. But he apparently didn't feel free to share all of his feelings with me.

One thing he did write was that he did not want me to come to Ecuador as a single worker. Why he said this I didn't know: Perhaps he thought that I felt it would help our relationship. Or maybe it was because he knew Betty had suggested the idea to me. But after witnessing how unhappy and lonely some of the single women were, and watching Jim's and Betty's heartache, he believed that my coming would only cause more problems.

He had nothing to fear; I had not even considered going as a single missionary. The only way I could see myself in Ecuador was as Pete's wife; that option seemed quite viable. Pete was pleased with the choices I was making about schooling and employment (though he expressed it only in his diary), since he probably saw my openness to joining him when the time was right.

After camp, I received an excellent job offer from the Navy for the fall, and accepted. When Pete later read of this in the jungles (letters were long delayed and sent in batches), he was thrilled for me. "God vindicated her over those who said she ought to have taken the job she was offered before she went to Camp Imadene. She sure is my girl, the girl for me, and I love her with all my being."

I figured that I would devote my next two years to working and perhaps study at Biola. Surely God would give Pete and me some direction in that time, I hoped. Perhaps Pete and Jim would contact the Aucas and establish the ministry in a way that would free them both to marry. By this point I at least felt a sense of direction for my life, without having to know precisely what Pete thought about our future.

Pete's departure for the jungles did not tear me apart as I had feared, probably because we were not saying good-bye in person again. Jim and Betty, however, had a very difficult time. Pete wrote in his diary and in his letters to me about their turmoil over yet another farewell:

> She is moody and quiet and obviously under a strain; Senora Arias says that she has come across Betty crying alone at night and wants Jim to do something about it. Jim said that last night he and Betty spent more time crying than talking and it was really a heart-rending time. Betty had received word of Ginny's engagement and of Dave's new baby and it just broke her up, I guess. All these joys came to her brother and sister younger than she is and still she has no *firm* promise, no engagement, and no prospected wedding-time.
>
> Well, there is one encouraging thing about it: our lives are becoming more and more decisive and the very basis of our lives is more and more resting on faith for *if* God isn't directing us (as we believe He is) we are sure fools to leave swell girls crying alone at night when there is nothing we'd rather do than be with them and take them as our own. It is either a joyous and triumphant walk of faith as single men or it is the worst mistake we ever made and a wasting of the best years of our lives without the love for which we were made. Thank God, we shall walk on in faith and God will triumph in us.

13
SHANDIA

*T*he day finally came to leave for the jungles—August 29, 1952. It also happened to be Pete's last day of camp counseling. "It was not till I was in the plane," he wrote, "... that I began to get excited about finally arriving—the rush of camp life hadn't given much time for anything."

Since thick vegetation had long ago consumed the Shandia airstrip, Pete and Dr. Tidmarsh flew to a nearby missionary station known as Pano. From there they would proceed on foot to Shandia, arriving later that day. Pano gave Pete his first glimpse of jungle life and his first encounter with the Quichua Indians.

> My first thought was, "Yes, I can love these people." The ink-colored designs on the women's faces interested me and the pitiful drape of the pleated section of their faded blue skirts. . . . Lots of children were about smiling shyly, and [women] suckling babies on big, tremulous breasts. . . . Heard T's first conversation in Quichua. Wondered how I would ever learn it.

In those days the women wrapped a piece of blue cloth around them, making a few pleats in front before tucking it in at the waist. On top they wore simple blouses left untucked, convenient for nursing babies. Lots of beads around the neck completed their outfit. The men usually wore long pants and shirts, or shorts. The Quichuas kept quite clean, bathing regularly in the rivers.

Next came the difficult, three-hour trek to Shandia on rain-drenched paths blocked with fallen limbs. "We slid through mud pools, over slimy roots and mossy logs well-soaked and slippery," Pete wrote. Low branches and tangling vines forced him to keep his head down, which also made it hard to see where he was going. "It was like some of the hikes we've had in the Cascades with the head bent low looking down, the neck stiff and shoulders sloped, striding away, slipping, sliding, but taking no notice of it, not resting very often." One lesson he learned quickly: "The mossiest trees often have the thickest thorns." He continued:

> We finally heard the roar of the Napo, saw the trees gradually thinning a bit, finally showing a bright green patch that looked like grass, and at last to step out into the open and see the three buildings [of Shandia] looking inviting and welcome in the late afternoon sun. . . . At my first glance the house looked spacious and comfortable, and thought how easily Olive and I could live in such a set up, feeling joy in the knowledge and anticipation. . . . Well at last I am here . . . tired . . . full of thankfulness to the Father who leads on. In reality, this is not an end but a beginning.

Now Pete at least knew it was *possible* to ask me to come and live with him there—sometime.

He and Jim (who arrived the next day) had to take many more jaunts over that slimy trail from Pano to Shandia, since all of their equipment for the station had to be carried in. After one trip he wrote of the guilt he felt as he walked, carrying nothing, while a little Indian boy carried a very heavy generator—a service for which he was paid. "It sure is hard to feel like a man in those circumstances, much less like a humble follower of Christ. I am not sure I am going to bow to the accepted in this, even if the accepted is in the minds of the Indians, but right now I'll walk softly and think long and pray."

Soon after they settled in Shandia, an older Indian man, Venancio, took Jim and Pete under his wing and told them he wanted them to be his "sons" and offered to teach them jungle life and lore. His kindness and immediate acceptance of them touched Pete. In the years that followed, Venancio remained true to his word.

A host of strange cultural experiences filled Pete's first days in Shandia. He welcomed every opportunity to be with the Indians and experience their way of life. One day he attended a Quichua wedding. Six people and a substitute bride danced to the sounds of a crude, three-string "violin" and the beat of a drummer, who also sang. (Pete and Jim later set Scripture passages and Bible truths to some of the Indian melodies instead of using Western hymnology.) Meanwhile the bridegroom, holding a white cloth in one hand, symbolically wiped away tears to make him appear woeful about the prospect of marriage. When word came of the true bride's arrival, another group ran out to meet her and threw a large red-and-white poncho over her head and face to conceal her identity. (The bride's wedding garments were community property, to be used over and over again.) Finally the veiled bride, her identity supposedly concealed, took her rightful place in the dance and the substitute left. At this point, the groom knelt before the father to ask for the bride.

In the midst of all the new cultural experiences Pete and Jim came face to face with a problem common to missionaries—conflicting claims as to what is authentic Christianity. One of their first guests was their neighbor, a priest. Pete described him as

> a bearded man in a long grey robe and a crucifix prominently displayed. He had come principally to try to get a guarantee from us that we wouldn't try to steal the children from his school and that we would treat him with respect. . . . He was clearly on the defensive.

Pete and Jim were seen as a threat to his mission. This was understandable as he had worked there for some time and no doubt saw it as his territory. Pete continued:

> To me it seems a tragedy that the Indians here have to decide between Catholics and Protestants when they don't understand the issues, and don't have the freedom to make a reasoned choice. They can hardly understand the gospel, much less the historical cleavage between two groups who apparently worship the same God. But in it all God is going to honor his name—He has to.

Jim and Pete were taken by Venancio to a three-hour pig killing and accompanying feast. Pete described in detail the various steps of the killing and butchering—something new for a city fellow. But some of their customs were hard to understand. At one point the male pig's genitals were cut in such a way as to create a long tube-like part, which was then handed to a boy, who chased people around and slapped them on the legs with this strange whip. Pete's only comment was: "It apparently is custom since everybody laughed and was good-natured about it."

Then the neighboring priest arrived. Surprised and threatened by the presence of Jim and Pete, he swished through the house in his clerical robes, warning the Indians that if they were Christians they would come to mass. But on Sunday the whole houseful attended Jim and Pete's service—even those who had gone to mass first.

The superior, out-of-touch attitude of this priest in all his regalia made a strong impression on Pete—especially in contrast to the crude penis-whipping custom he had just witnessed. The experience prompted him to carefully think through his strategy to reach the Indians:

> Jim and I will have to live in such a house [Indian-style] if we are to ever make a real impact with the people . . . (1) We've got to in order to really get their language— that is do their everyday tasks and speak their language in *their situations.* (2) We've got to live with them to make any impact on their social structure. Living their life with such modifications as are necessary for sanitation, etc., is the only way that the Indians will really copy important things for their own good. . . . We have to live like they do accepting their useful habits and give them only 10 useful hints for their lives instead of a 1000 which they can't assimilate, use, or copy. (3) Most basic of all was the feeling that in order to reach these for Christ we will have to be like them. We may lose some of the distant respect and love they have for a fatherly patron, but we will gain in being able to meet their problems with them and help them develop Christ-likeness in *their* environment—not give them an unrealistic goal of Christ-likeness in our controlled environment in their midst.

Within his first month of jungle living, Pete began to expand his vision to other Quichua population centers.

> [I] wondered about the idea of building several Indian- type houses in [those] areas and switching from place to place according as God leads and prospers. . . . It seems that with an itineration approach we will need an ultimate

base of operations, possibly Shandia itself. . . . I am impressed with the feasibility of the plan. I am in no way opposed to the mission-station approach as used here in Shandia but for Jim and me I feel it outside of God's plan. But for married couples with growing families it would be almost impossible to live "native" style.

He reasoned that a family would need a permanent place to live, and that permanency would require a school and a clinic. "I believe God has given it to us to break the mold, as far as I can tell, for the first time in the 25 year history of work in the northern Oriente."

There was much work to be done. Pete and Jim threw themselves into the most pressing task of clearing and leveling the deteriorated airstrip. Even with the Indians' help, it would be a month before the Mission Aviation Fellowship plane could land safely. For this entire time, the men had no contact with the outside world other than by two-way radio. Once again I had to wait for news from Pete. When the little MAF plane finally touched down and came to a stop, more than a hundred Indians joined in the celebration—especially those who had worked so hard alongside Pete and Jim. They were all pleased with their accomplishment. Now Pete and Jim could have meat, vegetables, candy, peanut butter, and best of all, their long-awaited letters from home.

But they had little time to rest on their laurels. The next few months were filled with fixing up the old buildings, constructing new ones, setting up and running the boys' school, and caring for the medical needs of the Indians. Trouble arose almost immediately at the school. Pete and Jim had to mediate between the frustrated children, their parents, and an Ecuadorian teacher who proved to be incompetent. Often the young missionaries hiked all day over trails and through rivers to help Indians in need—giving medicine for fevers, assisting with a difficult birth, or trying to save the life of a snake bite victim. After weeks of running from crisis to crisis, Pete and Jim realized this was not their idea of the life of an itinerant evangelist.

Pete described the first time he went with Dr. Tidmarsh (who visited on and off for a week or ten days at a time) to attend a delivery. "As it was the first birth I had seen it was intensely engaging though primitive in the extreme." Darkness had fallen by the time they reached the house. Their clothes were soaked from fording a river on the way. Since the baby had not yet arrived, the local midwife gave them two bamboo boards to lie on while they waited. The chill in the air— exacerbated by their wet clothes—and the inflexible boards kept them from sleep. They tried sitting on logs next to a smoky fire, but it gave off no heat to warm or dry them.

> In company with two mangy skeleton-ribbed dogs we sat listening to the whine of the crickets, the strange goose-like honking of the "cucupitsey," the occasional waking cry of a child, the creaking of the bamboo as someone rolled over, and the periodic moans of the woman which rose shrilly to a short scream.

As her labor pains increased, the young woman "rose to her knees and reached for the vine-rope which hung from the ceiling above, intertwining her hands in the rope and lifting her body when the pains came." Finally the baby began its descent. The midwife gave a word and the whole household "woke up and moved sleepily to the corner and stood peering over the curtain—privacy is a word and concept unknown." Venancio then went to the young woman, "grasped the girl by the shoulders and began shaking her violently which he continued until the baby arrived, dropping half onto the banana leaves and half on the earthen floor." It was a breech delivery. They cut the cord with the sharp edge of a bamboo stick. Then the midwife filled her mouth with water and spat it out over the baby for washing.

"There are several actions that I can't explain," Pete wrote afterward.

They prepared a drink for the girl by scraping the claw of a sloth and mixing the powder with water. . . . in the last stages of labor both the midwife and Venancio blew on the top of the girl's head, pressing their mouth down into the tousled black hair. And finally while waiting for the placenta they brought in a foot-long stick and stuck it in the ground right in front of her.

Pete and Jim witnessed death as well as birth in the jungle, attending their first two Indian funerals in the same week. Pete referred to them as "funeral celebrations." The first was for an older Indian man; the second for a baby who had died of a fever because the parents would not allow Jim and Pete to give it injections. The mourners' eerie death wail frightened Pete, and the "wakes" presented an awkward combination of hopelessness for the wailing family, and hilarity for the guests. All night they sat around, playing games and drinking. To keep awake, they tossed around a burning ball of kapok (a silky substance found in certain trees) soaked in kerosene. The idea was to throw it quickly before it burned one's hands. The Indians' thick, leathery hands gave them more protection than pale, thin-skinned Pete.

Death from snake bites occurred more often than they had expected, and without serum death was inevitable. Pete once wrote me of the helplessness he and Jim felt as they watched the onset of hemorrhaging, swelling, and finally death of an Indian for whom they did not have the necessary serum. Snakes were to be feared as they frequently struck without warning.

With all the awesome responsibility the men felt in these

life-and-death situations, they learned to temper their idealism of reaching entire Indian tribes for Christ with the reality of living with them, crying with them, and trying to be all things to them so that they might win them. They depended heavily on the Lord and on each other for support.

Before long they realized they did not have time to explore deeper into the jungles for other tribes, as they had planned. They had to limit their trips to either a day's walk from Shandia or to other stations just a few days away. On one occasion they came across a small populated area up the Napo River toward the Andean foothills that showed potential as an outpost. There they met a friendly group of Quichuas who had never before seen a missionary. They seemed happier and busier than those around Shandia. Pete and Jim decided that the area's higher elevation and its exquisitely beautiful, steep gorge with deep green water would make a desirable retreat location. They dreamed of one day building a house there as a getaway spot and as a base for outreach.

Pete never mentioned the Aucas in his diary during that first year in the jungles. Nor did he write much about me, other than occasional memories of our days together. Instead, he began to express his feelings and his love for me directly in personal letters. My fear that the distance between us would undermine our relationship proved to be unfounded. Even though letters arrived in batches, and many of our questions and answers crossed in the mail, our relationship grew stronger. God was answering my prayers.

His diary does show, however, that his love for Christ deepened during this time. He wrote of the "honest freedom I have to use the word 'love' in worship—it's becoming so that I need the word now and I can't get along without it."

A line from an old devotional song stirred him to greater service:

"Oh Master, lead me to the door. / Pierce this now willing ear once more. / Thy hands are freedom; let me stay / with Thee to toil, endure, obey." Yes, it's a glorious slavery and I want my ear pierced again by the kindest Master a slave could serve. I have been thinking today of the assertiveness of the Psalms; for example, "My heart is fixed, my heart is fixed, I will sing and give praise unto Thee" and "I will love Thee, Oh Lord, my strength" and "I shall not be moved." The thing is I feel that the future is so definitely out of my hands and in God's that assertiveness about it finds no place in my praise and appears only like self-confidence. But this can be over-done, and I am guilty of it.

Pete trusted in the Lord, but he also wrestled with discouragement at times. "Obedience at all costs" sounded good on paper, but everyday living put Pete to the test. The very people for whom he prayed, longed, and would give his life to reach for Christ, sometimes brought out the worst in him. The question of his gifts and abilities resurfaced as he struggled with practical duties of building or making repairs. He saw this issue as a spiritual battle and a basic problem in his mental makeup. On January 25, 1953, he wrote,

I am a slave in great areas of my life to what people think of me or better to my estimation of what they think. . . . the daily routine things I do only to gain their estimation and/or so that I shall stand in fair balance with their appraisal of Jim. I was stung badly the other day when [an Indian called me] a "wawa" [child] as I was trying to fix a gun. He said that Jim was the one that knew about guns. He repeated it this morning when I couldn't play the Jew's harp when asked. These things plague my mind and I really have to fight to gain victory over my spirit. The thing is there is a lot of truth in what he says and others recognize it and laugh, which hurts.

I am now taking all the opportunities to fix and repair things that I can so as to gain a knowledge of useful, practical things. This will help, but it doesn't hit the root of the problem which is that I am making as a basis for my judgment of my spiritual progress and acceptance here the opinion of men and I am cast down when they estimate me for what I am. But it is all wrong. God does not need a perfectly-trained, perfectly-acceptable, perfectly-capable person to do His work well. He tells us Himself that He doesn't need but the voices of children and babes, and that He doesn't do His work by our estimates of power or might or preparedness, but *"By My Spirit."*

He has encouraged me this afternoon to believe that He will use this "wawa" to His glory even though I look young and act young and can't shoot a gun or play a Jew's harp. I take God's encouragement to Jeremiah when he protested of being too young as me: "Say not I am a child; for thou shalt go to whomsoever I shall send thee and whatsoever I command thee thou shalt speak. *Be not afraid of them* for I am with Thee to deliver thee, saith Jehovah."

Although he believed in his heart that God did not need a "perfectly-capable person," Pete found it hard to accept on a daily basis. Six weeks after the above entry, he wrote once again of his discouragement. He wanted to bring honor and glory to God, but again felt oppressed by his

astounding inability along practical lines. (I note that I almost fear the building of the new house for I know it will show up ineptitude to all—I feel I could do it if only everybody wasn't watching me and noting my childishness.) Yet over the years God will square all that away.

132

And even in these years if I am misevaluated (due to the Indians' incomplete criteria) and misunderstood yet by God's grace I shall serve them and love them and labor in prayer for them.

To further compound his depression, Pete came down with malaria in late February 1953. He had to be flown out of the jungles and finally to Quito to recuperate, taking him out of commission for three weeks. He worried that the breakdown of his health, combined with his impracticality, were making him a hindrance in the jungle work. He recalled that some of his elders at home had predicted exactly this outcome.

Pete was not alone in his times of discouragement, however. Jim also struggled with his self-image. In July 1952, before he left for the jungles, Jim had written:

> Marveled at my inner weakness yesterday. Felt miserably unworthy to be here as an "administrator of the mysteries of God." Strange that I should—evidently for life—be put to such close contact with Pete and Betty whom I feel are far my intellectual superiors. Spanish studies, for instance. When Betty first arrived and saw Pete and I were studying at the same level, she said, "How did you get so far behind?"—that Pete should be up with me. And now she is competing with us both, right along in the same material! They are both able to correct my grammar and pronunciation, and seem to be able to apply tense rules so much easier than I. Felt weepy and useless yesterday at noon, swept with waves of envy and defeated wonderings about such things.[1]

A few days later he wrote about his feeling of unworthiness in comparison with Betty:

> I sense that I am not her better in anything. She is fine in her feelings, I am gross. She is settled in her thinking

about things ... I have to puzzle it slowly through making blunders and contradictions.... She knows the Spanish word for *tawdry*: I never heard of it. She can do a Spanish lesson faster and better.... In short, I see that she is my superior, and it frightens me.

Can I bear competition with that sort of woman all my life? And to her, I dare say, it never occurs that her efficiency makes me feel like I'm being beaten, and can't help it, just *can't help it.* I have seen husbands who are excelled by their wives and what piteous things they are, how out of place! Is that what her self-security, calmness, ability, and purity are going to make me when we marry? Great God in heaven, don't allow it! If only she didn't make me feel so small, if only she had had some great defeat in ignorance ... something that would make one feel at least morally her equal, yet I could not love her if she had, I fear....

I know it would help to talk to her, but can't bear to think of speaking of this thing in daylight when she could see me cry. She wouldn't believe me ... I don't usually display any humility that would suggest I felt myself her lesser. But I do. I know she would assure me that she didn't feel that way at all and that she didn't sense any superiority.... But there it is—and I'm none the happier for having written it....

Oh, if only she felt that she could tell me she loved me and why, perhaps that would bolster me somehow.... If only she could come to *me* instead of my having always to go to her, letting her control, having to follow so many times when I feel that I should be leading. But what is to be done? She *can't,* simply can't do otherwise until engagement—says it just has to be that way now. My God, what a vise I'm in.[2]

134

Jim and Pete had different kinds of gifts, which provided balance in the work. But they both had trouble accepting their limitations, and often compared themselves to each other or to Betty, with debilitating results. They were bumping up against a hard truth: that life goes on, even after one has heard and answered God's call—to the mission field or anywhere else. Everyday duties, personal struggles and relational issues continue, and must not be ignored or minimized. However, in spite of the difficulties—and there were more to come—the young missionaries managed to keep their ultimate goals in sight.

14
ENGAGED

*A*fter six months in the jungles, Pete and Jim saw that the Indians' greatest need, apart from salvation, was for medical help. The homeopathic remedies they had learned from Dr. Tidmarsh proved ineffective against many tropical diseases, especially malaria. They needed "wonder drugs" such as sulfa and penicillin. Pete's attempts to help the sick, as well as his own bout with malaria, made him wish he'd had more medical training. In his letters to me he suggested that I think more seriously about applying to the Biola School of Missionary Medicine.

I had already begun to consider that option. In the summer of 1952, I had met the school's director, Leone Soubirou, and explained my situation, as well as my uncertain future. She was very supportive. Since most missionary candidates had either attended Bible school or Bible college, my two years of university did not fully satisfy this program's admission requirements. But because she understood that the Brethren did not require formal Bible training, she agreed to accept the commendation of my church elders, along with a firm assurance that I would indeed go to the field. I could apply as soon as I knew I was going to Ecuador.

I thanked God for her encouragement. My job provided the tuition money, but I still needed the commendation from my elders. Here is where things got sticky.

I knew Pete didn't want me to go to Ecuador (nor did I want to go there) as a single woman. He wanted me to wait until *he* was ready to marry me. Now, as I tried to decide when to apply to Biola, I found myself in an awkward situation. I would need to contact the elders soon. I couldn't honestly ask for their commendation as a single missionary; but since Pete had only given me vague assurances about the timing of our future, neither could I allude to our possible marriage.

I had no doubt that my latest "understanding" with Pete was a real commitment. Somehow, in spite of an eighteen-month separation punctuated by scattered batches of mail, our love had patched its wounds and even grown stronger. But I worried that we might have to wait even longer to marry, because Pete had not fulfilled the goals that had caused him to sever our relationship in the first place. He and Jim had their hands full at Shandia, treating the Indians for disease, managing the school, and constructing several new buildings. They had not taken the long trips deeper into the jungles as they had hoped. Pete didn't even mention the Aucas anymore. I remembered with fear Pete's earlier statement about needing five to ten years to accomplish all they wanted to do as single men. Nevertheless, I decided that now was the time to ask him for a more specific word about our future. I dropped the letter into the mailbox with a quick prayer for God's guidance.

Before receiving my letter, Pete wrote to tell me that Jim and Betty had gotten engaged. He said that the past year had been difficult for them and that their engagement would make life easier. They would marry in a year. I snickered at the word "difficult." They, at least, could see each other. And, after all, hadn't they chosen that "sacrificial" way of life—Jim as a celibate, and Betty, obeying at any cost? I recalled Jim's adamant insistence that he serve God as a single man. Now all those strong convictions had come tumbling down. I wondered how their engagement would affect Pete, who I knew tended to follow Jim's lead in matters such as this.

I didn't have to wonder long—not long, at least, for those days. A month later I received the following letter from him:

Quito, Ecuador
March 4, 1953
Dearest Olive,

The main purpose of this letter is to ask you officially and deliberately to marry me. As you well know I have loved you increasingly for several years and have received many and varied assurances that this is the will of God for me. So that I would love above all things to share my life with you and believe that we could honor God by our being one. I appreciate more than you can know the fact that you have waited for me and stood by even when others gave you no encouragement and would like to honor your faithfulness and fulfill my joy by marrying you. I would count it a joy to care for you and if God should be pleased to give us a family there is nothing that would give greater happiness to me. In the mercy of God I really believe that these things are ahead of us, dear, and if you feel the same heart toward me, as I believe that you do, then I think that we can look forward to our future lives with great expectation for new and rich experiences and by our living together an increased understanding of the character of God.

I want to ask you now, darling, in order that every thing should be clear for you in your mind as you think about your future training at Biola or elsewhere. Then too

I would be glad to make it official and public at any time that best suits you and this I am sure will satisfy a lot of people's curiosity and deliver you from a lot of needless talk and misunderstanding of motives. So if you are agreed, as soon as I hear from you we can begin to think about how you would like to announce it. I think that after I hear from you I will write immediately to my folks telling them what is going to happen and asking them to help you with all the arrangements. I will be just as frank and open as possible and I am sure they will be willing to help; in fact anxious to get in on it. I think I will ask Dad to act in my place at any public announcement if that is needed and I think that he will get a bang out of it.

I will leave the matter of the ring with you, dear, to do as you like. I have money here which I brought from the States that I have saved for just this purpose so I don't want you to feel that I am taking money that has been sent to me for the Lord's service for this. Since sending the jewelry from here is out of the question I have two alternatives: (1) to send the money straight to you and let you choose the ring and make all the arrangements or (2) to send the money to Dad and ask him to handle it in consultation with you. I think he would like to do it and feel kind of a pride in doing it if you would like him to. Since he has the insurance of about 70% of Seattle's jewelry he knows all the best buys and the best guys to get them through with least unnecessary expense. So that I think that he would be able to get the money's worth if you would like him to do it. He got Ken and Helena's ring for them and I think it worked out very well. You would have to tell him the size, etc., and what type you wanted, either solitaire or one large stone with two smaller ones flanking it, like Helena, or just whatever appeals to you. I personally prefer the three-stone rings in a nice setting but I will leave it with you to do just as you dreamed of. I know there will be some people who think that you ought not to have a ring at all since it is needless expense and that you are headed to a life of sacrifice which ought to begin now, but most of these people don't have a very realistic view of the mission field. I would like so much to get you a ring that you may wear and treasure for the rest of your life that I do not care what they say and I just think you will have to steel yourself against any snide remarks like "looks like business is good on the mission field" or any such and kid 'em right back.

So I will await word from you, little one, as to whether you "want me" and if perchance so, then what you think about all the possible arrangements. You are perfectly at liberty to announce right away, hold it off till June or the summer or just whatever you say since you are the "boss" as you well know. Anyway I am happy in thinking about it and will be praying for you in it. . . .

At one level, his letter made me very happy; I knew what my answer was. But at another, it seemed cold and restrained, far from my girlhood dreams of a romantic proposal. He used unsentimental words such as "official" and "deliberate." Other phrases sounded more like an awards presentation than a marriage proposal. He wanted to make it official and public so I could apply to Biola, which is basically what I had asked him for. But now it seemed too much like a contract rather than an impassioned plea for the hand of a woman he adored. If he missed me, he didn't say. I appreciated his spiritual insight that our life together would help us understand God's character, but where was the romance? How romantic would it be to choose a ring with his father?

Other questions came to mind. Why hadn't he called from

Quito to talk with me in person about such an important decision? Why hadn't he given me any idea of a possible wedding date? And perhaps most important, whatever happened to the Aucas? They had been the main reason that Jim and Pete had resisted marriage. Why did he not mention them? Were they no longer thinking of trying to reach the Aucas?

Even as I asked these questions, I felt guilty. How ungrateful I was. Hadn't God worked and answered my prayers? Why was I so negative? Deep down I think I still feared Jim's influence on Pete. It seemed easy to speculate that because Jim was engaged, it was now okay for Pete to ask me. I hated that Pete was so far away at such an important time. In person it would have been so different, so much more real, so much more assuring. But amid all my questions, I remembered how deeply Pete had loved me before his decision to go to Ecuador, and I knew I loved him even if I couldn't understand everything just now.

After mailing the letter to me, Pete had noted the proposal in his diary, thanking God

> for the comfort of the knowledge that she will [say yes]. I have perfect peace on asking her for I have never doubted since coming here that she was God's choice for me and have only wondered when it would be wise to make our agreement an engagement. The time is now since she will need the assurance as she plans for Biola next year and it will make her position understandable to the folks at home. So I rejoice—the time is now.

Twenty days after I received his proposal, he had my answer. His diary expressed his excitement:

> Olive will marry me! And we plan our engagement as soon as possible. Hallelujah—I am really happy and warmed inside at the prospect. She will "do me good and

not evil all the days of her life," I know and will be an excellent helpmeet. No details as to the engagement yet; mail here is slow!!

Pete's father officially announced the engagement at a church missionary meeting. Though I found engagement to an absentee fiancé hard to grasp, it was nevertheless an exciting time. I actually did enjoy going with Pete's father to pick out the kind of ring Pete wanted. It had a lovely diamond between two smaller ones. Pete did not hear of the public announcement for almost a month because of the mail. I couldn't even call him to tell him I had the ring. Sometimes I felt I was engaged to a dream. But I tried to make him feel part of the occasion by sending pictures of me with the ring and with all our friends. Upon receiving these, he described in his diary his "thrill" that our engagement was official and that he could now share the pictures with his friends. From then on his letters, in which he could finally speak openly about marriage, helped to dispel my fears. We hadn't yet set a wedding date, but at least I knew I was marrying Pete and joining him in Ecuador. Within a short time I received the elders' commendation and was accepted at Biola for the fall of 1953.

Pete had proposed to me from Quito while recovering from a bad case of malaria, the first in a series of health setbacks. After regaining his strength, he returned to Shandia and buried himself in the work. He and Jim were building a house for the McCullys, who had recently arrived in Ecuador and decided to move to Shandia after their language study in Quito. The ongoing medical needs of the Indians consumed much of their time. Amid the physical labor, they also struggled to learn Quichua, the Indians' unwritten language. But they were making progress.

In early summer the men received an emotional boost in the form of a propane-powered refrigerator, flown into the station in three separate flights. Once they managed to assemble the pieces, they reveled in their first batch of ice cubes. Maybe life in the jungles wasn't so bad, they must have thought. Soon the house would be completed and the McCullys would join them in Shandia. Then perhaps they could take their long canoe trips to find more Indians. "Hurry the rest of our preparation now, Lord," Jim wrote in his journal. "With all this planning and building going on, I will certainly enjoy our dreamed-of itineration in the forest."[1]

Unfortunately, their days of "preparation" were far from over. The heavy rains of June changed everything.

June 14, 1953, was a "day to be remembered," Pete wrote in his diary. Torrential rains had caused the Napo River to rise to an alarming level. The roaring rampage had sliced away huge chunks of the seventy-foot cliff, toppling several buildings into the river. The edge of the cliff had now moved dangerously close to Pete and Jim's house and also the new McCully house. Though neither of the men showed discouragement in their journals or letters, they knew they were facing a major setback. In the next few weeks, they dismantled and moved the McCullys' new house back to a safer location and began to build again. But the rain often forced them inside, where they continued their language study, wrote in their journals, kept up with correspondence—and waited.

The rains not only affected Jim and Pete, but also Nate Saint, an MAF pilot who, with his wife, Marj, had just returned from furlough. Nate had flown a new plane to Ecuador from California. The heavy clouds and pouring rain in the jungles, however, grounded Nate in the mountains for days.[2]

Jim was still reeling over the implications of his engagement to Betty. He realized he could no longer be the idealist and counsel young men to follow his example of singleness. He wrote,

Little did I know for what I dealt in those days [when] I said I was willing for celibacy—nothing did I know about the power of love for a woman, I believe. So help me, God, I did not know! Had I been aware of what I should feel this morning as the rain falls heavily out of a low sky, I doubt if I would have made any sort of vow of willingness to stay single.[3]

On another rainy day Jim continued his confession:

I never knew that love would be so intense for me, that it could be constant and strong enough to leave one with this emptiness day and night, in whatever activity. Pete gives me patter about controlling with the will the undisciplined emotions, but it is nonsense. I used to think that, too, that it was all a matter of willing not to be overcome of love that would keep one balanced and protected from "getting silly" over a woman. But what happens when the will itself is affected? The will is stronger even than the emotions of wanting. But I can see no way for marriage during this year. God is giving us what we asked for, single lives, and freedom to move in the Oriente. But here we are building houses. . . . Everything says wait—rain, materials lacking, language study calling—but love for her inside me says wait for nothing.[4]

The tables had been turned: now Pete had become the advocate of continence.

Jim and Betty decided to get married in January. Jim talked over their decision with Pete and later recorded Pete's reaction:

He is completely at rest in the whole matter, saying that the will of God for us goes right on, married or unmarried, and that he does not at all feel as though I were leaving him out "in the cold," as some shall [say] if I marry first. On the contrary, he feels that we should be married at different times, as it would complicate housing. . . . So I will write Betty tonight."[5]

Jim's concern about Pete's response might suggest that he felt guilty about marrying after all his rhetoric about singleness. And besides, out of all the many things he had hoped to do as a single man, none had been accomplished.

Meanwhile, the rains refused to subside over the next few weeks. The latest downpour had continued for four days solid. The Napo River was rising to a dangerous level—for the second time in less than two months. On the morning of the fifth day, Jim and Pete knew they were in for big trouble. Pete wrote:

On July 30, all that we knew of Shandia went down the river! . . . We worked on the dictionary till nearly noon, had an early lunch and watched anxiously as the water rose. About noon [the cliff] started to fall . . . and by 1:30 it had taken the aerial posts and the flowering stump from the front of the house. After a brief radio contact we abandoned all the house, putting the equipment in the school; we felt numb and could still hardly believe it would fall. Just about as the cliff reached the front ditch we began to tear the house apart—the walls, floor, screening, etc. and we worked till all the Indians had left for fear and until the porch was gone. A great crowd of Indians came [from around the area] and helped in the gray, rainy afternoon. Jim then guided the moving of the lumber next to the old foundation and I began to dismantle the clinic, putting all the stuff in the school kitchen. [Tearing up the clinic was the hardest part of all because] we had built it and it was the newest and best of the buildings. We saved a lot of the floor timbers, cupboards, doors, etc. and we pulled the house over by rope to try to save the house poles, but we lost all of them—there was not time to save all the stuff.

As we were working on the clinic, we saw the house fall and the Indian women set up the death wail. It was then late afternoon and raining, but it was apparent that the school was going to go, so we moved, with great help from all the Indians, our stuff from the school to the site we had just cleared and marked off for the professor's house .... Then, at seven, nightfall, we went into the school kitchen [a separate structure from the school itself] to await developments.... About nine the school began falling and we knew our stuff was in danger, so with Venancio [and several other Indians] we worked six long hours moving our equipment—it was a nightmare of stumbling in the pitch black, stepping on nails, crushing our shins against stumps and fallen trees, staggering under 100-lb. loads in deep mud and lurching as we stepped in sink holes to our knees, shivering from the drenching rains and the cold wind off the river.

The roar of the river was deafening, the ground would shake as huge chunks of cliff and trees fell away. We were sick at heart to see everything drenched, and the sight of Dr. [Tidmarsh]'s priceless Quichua vocabulary [notes] strewed all over the ground and tracked in the mud was the saddest of all. Just before 3 [A.M.] we finished . . . and headed off to Vicente's house with a blanket, where we warmed out by a fire and lay down for a couple hours' sleep.

Before six [A.M.] we heard Venancio shouting again and we raced across the swollen Churu Yacu [stream] up the airstrip to find the school kitchen had gone during the night [as well as] all the play field and that the cliff was now only 30 feet from where we had put the stuff during

146

the night. So again we raced against time to move it again, this time with a lot of help, cutting a trail straight back thru the jungle and having Venancio build an aluminum-roofed shelter. Venancio and Luis, during the night, had moved the refrigerator back to safety by putting planks down and pushing it along, but somewhere back of the school kitchen we must have lost Ed [McCully]'s barrel with all his kitchen stuff.

About 10 o'clock that morning the river began to ease off a little, though we spent the rest of the day moving the stuff [farther from the river] to dry [it] out . . . and get it repacked. . . . On Saturday we set up our 16' x 16' tent, where we have been living ever since. . . .

We saw that in one stroke God had wiped out the station . . . and rendered McCullys' house, which [now] stood about 13 yards from the cliff edge, relatively useless. We had lost our five houses, the play field, over a hundred meters of the airstrip—in a word, everything was gone of the physical plant and it was a destruction more complete than we had imagined possible. Most of our equipment was saved, but the Indians stole a good deal (machetes, axes, shovel, salt, cement and oddments); the biggest loss was the barrel of Ed's with all his kitchen equipment. . . .

The Indians called it a disaster. The priest proclaimed it God's punishment on the Protestants. In Pete's mind, "it provided us a priceless opportunity to demonstrate the Christian attitude toward tragedy."

What was God trying to tell them about the future of Shandia? During the night of the first flood, Pete had written, "We felt the destruction was so complete that God must have had something else in mind than only the trying of our patience." (And this was *before* the rest of Shandia's buildings had been destroyed.)

After the second flood wiped out everything, Pete reflected that its timing appeared to be significant in regard to God's will for Shandia. He wrote:

(1) A week before [the flood] we had come to a strange deadlock with Eladio [the school teacher at Shandia] over his salary—thus we were free from a binding contract with him.

(2) We were just poised to launch an intensive building program for the summer months. . . . In just that moment God carried away everything, saving us the expense and labor of doing what we had planned.

(3) God had recently tested us [after the first flood] on our willingness to rebuild so that it seemed unlikely that only this was in his mind.

(4) The day before the flood Jim told me he felt that the time had come for him to get married and that the previous week he had gone to Dos Rios to discuss the date with Betty. He felt that the rhythm of their love was reaching its conclusion, accelerated as it had been since last January and that biologically and with the view of the needs of the work in Shandia it was now time to get married. He felt that our vision of traveling would not be hindered and that all that he had said about exploring as single men did not mitigate the feeling he had that now was the time for marriage.

I replied with honest feeling that if he felt now was the time he ought to go ahead. . . . it is impossible for me to feel that I will be left "high and dry"; God will fulfill his promises to me whatever happens. I said, however, that if we were able physically and mentally to do traveling on a large scale in the next few months, then immediate marriage would probably be a hindrance, but that if we found that it was better to do a little at a time then his marriage would probably not cut down our efficiency. His plan was to build a small house on the cement foundation left over from Ed's first house, [but the] next day that platform went down the Napo. God seemed to be saying to Jim to wait a bit as to marriage and to get moving in itineration.

If indeed God was directing them to leave Shandia, it would be a hard decision for Pete to make. "God has given me deep love for the Indians and it would be terrible to have to leave them," he wrote.

I could not think of permanently pulling out of Shandia. My meditation in these days has been on the "way of love" from 1 Cor. 13 and the exercise has been to examine my attitude when dealing with any Indians who come to the house to see if [my love for them] is evident and flowing. I will never be known among them as a clever carpenter or builder or engineer, but I would like to be their lover for Christ's sake—that is something I can be if by God's help I set myself to be.

Ed McCully had joined Jim and Pete to help after the flood. Shortly thereafter Dr. Tidmarsh arrived to survey the scene and talk about the future. They decided that now was the time for Jim, Pete, and Ed to venture into the southern area of the Quichua territory. There they would search for Indians who had not heard of Christ, and establish a new outpost. Jim and Pete had spent the last year rebuilding Shandia for one main reason: to seek out unreached Indians. Ironically, its destruction paved the way for their trip. Betty stayed in a tent in Shandia to watch over the equipment while the men were away.

Rather than give any exciting descriptions of the adventure, Pete made his usual list of observations:

It was a total of 21 days, 15 of which were spent in canoe travel. Salient features of the trip were: (1) since it was our first survey trip it taught us loads on how to travel; (2) gave us our first *canoe* trip of any length; (3) it was the first evangelical trip ever made into that area and we found many who have never heard of the name of Jesus; (4) we investigated areas where there was interest in school, such as Bella Vista, Montalvo and received invitations from them; (5) we came into contact with a significantly different Quichua dialect; (6) Ed got his first experience in camping and trail work; (7) it became evident that we will never reach the Bobanaza from Shandia; (8) there are far more Jivaros in the area than we had thought and it may be one of us will have to learn Jivaro.

The men agreed to accept the Indians' invitation to Bella Vista, also known as Puyupungu, which would allow them to reach many Indians along the Puyu River. But who would go to start the work there and open a school? The McCullys, being new, needed to be at the established work at Shandia, where they could have their first exposure to jungle life and language study. There was no question in Jim's mind, however: He and Betty would marry in October and move to Puyupungu. Pete would stay in Shandia and begin the building of temporary housing for himself and the McCullys. The long-range plan was to rebuild Shandia and ask Jim's father to come and help with the permanent construction.

On September 29, 1953, Pete wrote:

A very busy day—Jim and Betty left for Quito this morning to be married the 8th of October. They are sure happy and manifest the same tendencies as any newly engaged couple: shy holding of hands or the nudging of each other, the desire to talk about the other and put them in a desirable light ... the desire to be alone, the going over and over of wedding plans, ideas, home designs, etc. It is wholesome, though, and there is something pleasing and infectious about it. They are not expecting anything but a civil wedding so I don't expect to go out for it. They have waited long enough—a year and a half since Betty came to Ecuador—and the wait has allowed them to fulfill their respective goals as single workers; they will make an excellent couple for this type of work.

15
COMING HOME

Back in Seattle, Pete's father had received a telegram from Ecuador during the first week of August, 1953: "FLOOD DE-STROYED SHANDIA. SAVED STUFF. ALL WELL. INFORM PORTLAND. LOVE PETE." Not until a few weeks later did Pete's batch of letters arrive with all the details. I couldn't fathom the destructive power of that river, or even the torrential tropical rains. I knew it didn't compare with the soft drizzles of the Northwest. With Shandia in ruins, I wondered how the timetable for our marriage would be affected. Pete had just left on the three-week canoe trip as I began studies at Biola in Los Angeles. It would be a long wait for another letter.

The weeks passed quickly as I immersed myself in studies and part-time work in a nearby hospital. There was no time to brood over the delays in correspondence; in fact, I had gotten used to the long waits. I also appreciated having a group of students around me who shared common concerns about foreign missions. One woman was going to a primitive tribe in New Guinea much like those in Ecuador. Since she too had an absentee fiancé, we could relate to each other. I began to look at my difficult separation from Pete as an opportunity for spiritual growth. Reminding myself that I was now training for a jungle ministry also helped.

Pete's letter finally arrived, bringing news not only of his canoe trip, but also of Jim's and Betty's plans to marry in October—just a few weeks away. I was surprised, especially in light of Jim's previous indecision. In my mind, Pete had placed himself at the mercy of Jim's wavering for a long time. Now I knew he would feel released from his oath of singleness and talk to me about a wedding date. But I had eight months of studies ahead. Plus, Pete had urged me to go to language school in Costa Rica to avoid the distractions he had while studying Spanish. That would delay our marriage another six months. I wondered what he would say.

Sure enough, while Jim and Betty went to Quito for their wedding—a civil ceremony attended only by the Tidmarshes and the McCullys—Pete wrote his tentative plans for us in his diary: "In these days I have been thinking seriously for the first time of going home for our wedding next June, then taking in Wycliffe in the summer and going to Costa Rica's language school in the fall. That way Olive could go straight to the jungles." At that point he said nothing to me about a wedding.

Pete spent the month of October alone in Shandia, rebuilding the station. The Elliots were enjoying their honeymoon in Panama and Costa Rica before packing for Puyupungu, and the McCullys would join Pete later. Unlike his first discouraging attempt at construction, Pete found the new building project exhilarating. This time he managed to do many tasks he thought he could never do:

> I have had my house built, Eladio's room fixed, Venancio's kitchen fixed, the school land cleared, and school benches and chairs made. . . . It is surprising what joy and pleasure I have had in building my little two-room house. . . . it took only four or five days. . . . It is *very*

comfortable and it is *pure luxury* to have a place to yourself—a bed, desk and chair to yourself without always being under observation. Best of all it aids in leading a disciplined life, things are in a convenient place, and privacy for prayer is now possible. I have begun again to add to my file system on the New Testament, something I haven't done since coming to Ecuador. And I am happy inside myself to be getting things done in an orderly way again; there is no question but that it is the way I was meant to live, with a regular bed time, evenings free for study and a full hour or more devotional time in the morning.

His grasp on the unwritten Quichua language improved as he listened to Indians telling their stories. He spent long hours going over New Testament accounts with an Indian, learning Quichua expressions and constructions that became valuable in Bible translation and teaching. He was getting closer to having "chatty conversations on any subject."

When the McCullys moved down a few weeks later with their son, Stevie, Pete enjoyed himself even more. Now he could take advantage of Marilou's home cooking. He also appreciated her care when he was sick.

In December, Cliff Peterson, a friend of Pete's from Seattle, visited Shandia. One night, when rain prevented Nate Saint from flying Cliff back to Shell Mera, Cliff, Pete, and Nate talked about the Aucas. Pete responded to their conversation in his diary:

The Auca problem is a grave and solemn one; an unreachable people who murder and kill with a hatred which causes them to mutilate the bodies of their victims. It came to me strongly then that God is leading me to do something about it and a strong idea and impression came into my mind that in the six month period before I go

154

home (for I have fully decided to go [back to the States to marry Olive in June]) I ought to devote the majority of my time to collecting linguistic data on the tribe and make some intensive air surveys to look for Auca houses. I could easily establish myself in Ila [where Dayuma lived] and study there and still keep an eye on Shandia. . . . It comes to me strongly that I am the logical one to be burdened for I have some qualification for it that none else has . . . am still single . . . know both Quichua and Spanish . . . essential for gathering of linguistic data. . . .

I know that this may be the most important decision of my life but I have a quiet peace about it. Strangely enough I do not feel my coming marriage as prohibiting myself from being eligible for this service. I feel if pushed to it, Olive would rather have me die after we had lived together than to indefinitely postpone our wedding in the possibility that something fatal might happen. Our life has become one and I do not feel that God will separate us in our discernment of the will of God. I feel now only this: that in the six months after Christmas I ought to devote myself to the preparing of myself should God see fit to call me.

I have already written Olive a Christmas letter telling her that I am coming home for our wedding—she will be thrilled. I am too. . . .

So ended the ideal of service as a single missionary. Singleness—the issue that was once so important to Pete that he would abruptly cancel our relationship, the issue that led to a painful and lengthy separation—now no longer mattered.

Just after Pete sent that letter, his malaria recurred. A week later it struck again, more severely. Even large doses of drugs failed to alleviate his high fever and vomiting, which left him dangerously dehydrated and weak. Again he had to be flown to a mountain town, where a doctor and nurse from radio station HCJB met him and drove him to a hospital in Quito. Again he struggled with the accompanying depression and dejection, crying out to God for help. God heard his prayer and gave him a quietness of mind. The words "Be strong in the Lord and in the power of *his* might" comforted him.

"I had tried to buck up my courage and my faith but had forgotten that the only means of success is to do it in the power of *His* might," he wrote. "There is nothing but rest in His might which gives victory and there is nothing but failure and emptiness in trying to overcome discouragement without that rest. *His* might was enough; mine had been woefully insufficient."

At Biola, I felt lonely and depressed as I prepared to endure my first Christmas away from home. My small, dreary dorm room did nothing to boost my spirits. The spartan atmosphere made for good missionary training, I told myself. Ten days before Christmas, however, a familiar blue envelope from Ecuador in my mailbox rekindled my excitement. It was labeled DO NOT OPEN TILL CHRISTMAS on the back and front. I knew it had to be good news. How could I wait that long?

I managed to restrain myself until Christmas Eve, when I finally tore open the letter.

El Shandia, Ecuador
December 5, 1953

My darling,

MERRY CHRISTMAS! and eat lots of turkey for me. I have news for you, little one, to try and make this day away from home and your fiancé a happy one:

I AM COMING HOME FOR OUR WEDDING NEXT JUNE!!!!!

Did you read that? Would you like me to repeat it? I will gladly. I am coming home to be married to you in Seattle next June after you graduate from Med. School. Hallelujah. If you are half as excited as I am about it you won't be able to eat any Christmas turkey dinner. I am so happy to be able to tell you about it because I know it will mean a lot to you and to your folks. And if possible it will mean even more to me to be back with you again in Seattle with all our folks and we will be able to have a nice wedding of any style you plan among friends and familiar surroundings. So, my darling, I wish you every happiness for your holiday and I earnestly hope and pray that this may give you some added incentive to rejoice! FOR I LOVE YOU WITH ALL MY SOUL AND I WILL BE HOME TO MARRY YOU IN LESS THAN SIX MONTHS' TIME. D.V. [*Deo Volente,* which means God Willing].

Now for a few more details. I have been praying earnestly about coming home for the last several months and I have decided before the Lord that that is what I ought to do. I have been tempted to tell you in one of my recent letters but I thought I would save the news until today, Christmas, so that perhaps it might in some way make up for the fact that I cannot be with you. There are of course a number of reasons that have made me decide before the Lord to come home but certainly one of the foremost is just that I would like to give you the privilege of being married among all your friends and with your folks. And then of course surroundings would be a lot more familiar to you for our honeymoon there than in a South American country where everybody would be speaking an unfamiliar language. Of course it will have the added benefit of allowing me to see my folks and family which will be an added pleasure for me. But most of all it is to be with you in the old places and the familiar spots where I first began to love you.

I have talked of the possibility of my going home to my immediate fellow workers, that is, to Ed, Jim and Doc T. [Tidmarsh] and they are all in favor of my going. Even Doc T. said that he "warmly approved" in a letter he wrote the other day. I felt that it would only be fair to mention the idea to them so that they could measure in their minds what effects it would have on the work here. It will cause no problems or inconvenience here as far as we can see. But you are the first person to know definitely that I am coming for I wanted to surprise you with it first.

At present I am planning to follow through with a plan to go to the Language School with you in Costa Rica about the first of September where we will probably stay for about two terms, or six months, studying Spanish. I have heard most enthusiastic reports of the school and feel that it would probably give you the best introduction to Spanish, and then it will mean that when we get back to Ecuador we can come pretty well straight back into the jungles with you not having to spend a period of language study in Quito. . . . That would give us the summer at home in the States to enjoy a long honeymoon!! And further it will mean that I will be able to help you with the Herculean job of buying, packing and shipping all the equipment we will need. . . . So, my little one, I am so happy for both of us and I know that you will be too. IT WILL BE WONDERFUL TO SEE YOU AGAIN AND TO GIVE YOU ALL MY LOVE. Until then, merry Christmas and the happiest New Year of your life. Love, Pete.

It was better news than I ever would have imagined. Through tears of joy I read the letter again. Pete was actually coming home to marry me and take me down to Ecuador. My lingering fear that Pete would be influenced by Jim even to the timing of our marriage disappeared.

I couldn't have asked for a happier Christmas. In less than six months he would be home! After all my doubts, I now knew he had never stopped loving me. He was the same romantic Pete I had first fallen in love with. Why had we gone through those years of uncertainty? I wondered. Had this been God's way of "thrusting" Pete into the jungles and of shaping my desire to join him in Ecuador? I didn't know, but my excitement about Pete coming home eclipsed all my questions. I didn't even think about the Aucas or the possible danger to Pete. At that moment, only one thing mattered: God had kept our love alive. Surely he would guide our future together.

Pete enjoyed Christmas in Shandia with the McCullys (in their nearly completed house) and the Elliots, who had come from Puyupungu for a holiday. Immediately afterward, Pete and Jim and Ed hosted a men's Bible conference. Pete wrote:

> We are in the middle of the first young men's conference ever held among the Quichua tribe—it is a tremendous joy and great responsibility. About [40 fellows came] so our limited facilities are overcrowded. . . . This is really the first time that we have given instruction to believers . . . and it needs a different vocabulary than we use for the regular gospel messages. . . . I have followed the practice of writing out in full my main messages and getting help on translation of verses and ideas from various Indian fellows—that way I get far greater variety of expression and use a wider vocabulary.

Pete, the teacher, loved being back in his element.

The day after the conference Jim and Pete held a baptism, a first for them and the first in Shandia. Two Quichua girls were among the first believers there. Pete wrote:

159

It was a real thrill to baptize first Orqueña and Carmela in the cool pleasant water of the Talag. What perhaps was the most thrilling part of all was that a number of people also told us they wanted to be baptized. . . . We have prayed unceasingly for them, especially the school boys for many months. Oh God, thank you for this encouraging sign—it is worth all the heartache, fight and struggle. May God bring their desire to pass, *defeating the devil.*

When Cliff Peterson returned to the States, he told me about his time with Pete and mentioned their discussion about the Aucas. This was the first I had heard of the Aucas in a long time. Cliff said they had considered various strategies for reaching the tribe—even the possibility of sending a woman in first. "Better find out who they have in mind before you get married," he teased. I laughed, but on the inside I was afraid at the thought of the Aucas.

Pete's hope of moving down to Ila to live closer to the Aucas (mentioned in his December diary entry) never materialized. Instead, malaria attacked him again in February. Alone in Shandia at that time (the Elliots had returned to Puyupungu and the McCullys had gone to Quito for a few weeks), he decided to leave before the fever got too high. While recovering in Shell Mera, he thought about his health and his future:

I was burdened, however, with the possibility that I might not be able to return to Shandia with Olive. When I was sick again last December I felt the same. . . . I have never been really well here and have been seriously sick several times since coming. I asked the Lord then that if He wanted me to continue on in Shandia He would seal it to me by giving me good health in the remaining six months. This He has not seen fit to do for in less than two months I came down with malaria again in spite of taking the prophylaxsis [malaria prevention pill]. . . .

Again he asked God to reconfirm his call by giving him good health in the remaining months. His mind was filled with "fears that I might have to leave Jim and Ed alone in the work here, fears that they might also have to leave for health reasons, fears that Olive might not understand, and loneliness for her."

Amid his fear and doubt, an ill-timed letter arrived. A friend in Seattle told him some people in his church were criticizing him for using "the Lord's money" to go home for the wedding. His response?

They think I am coming home for health reasons instead of to marry Olive. God knows. No doubt at the back of their mind is the lingering doubt that I was in the will of God to leave at all and come here—I am sure Dad still doubts. When I came I felt this most strongly of all, that although my primary interest and gift was Bible teaching that I should do as Timothy was instructed, "do the work of an evangelist and make full proof of my ministry" until such time as God should raise up a Bible teaching ministry for me here in Ecuador or in other places, or I should return to the States for it. I feel just the same now—if God develops a work for me here, fine! If not and I return to the States or any other Latin American country for a teaching ministry, fine too. All I honestly want is the will of God. I believe I have walked in it so far and I believe God will guide me in it till death and not allow me to make mistakes!

I knew nothing of this criticism. Both of our parents favored his return home and never hinted that anyone else felt otherwise. (They knew others had criticized Pete, but said nothing because they didn't want to cast a shadow over our plans.) I eventually heard about it from Pete, however. He felt that people again misunderstood him, just as when he first decided to pursue missions. Fortunately, this time he had my support and that of both families.

Pete went back to Shandia as soon as he regained his strength. Though much construction remained to be done, in addition to completing repairs on the damaged airstrip, the school had resumed operation. The progress encouraged him. On Sundays the Indians packed out the schoolroom for the service; during the week the children's meeting continued to grow. God had answered their prayers to preserve the ministry at Shandia after the flood.

But other thoughts had begun to occupy the minds of the three men. That spring, Ed and Nate saw from the air the airstrip and ruins of Arajuno, a small, long-since-abandoned camp built by Shell Oil on the edge of Auca country. The men hoped that someday they could establish a station at this old camp to work with the Quichuas in the area, but also with the hope of making a contact with the Aucas. Without knowing where the Aucas were located, the men began moving one step closer to reaching them.

In late April, Jim's father arrived in Shandia, along with some valuable construction equipment, to help the three men rebuild the station. Jim had to take on the heavy responsibility of directing both the building program and the ministry to the Indians, since Pete was leaving for the States in a few weeks, Ed didn't yet know enough of the Quichua language, and Jim's father knew none. Jim had already spent his first seven months of marriage in Puyupungu, building that station and starting the school and the ministry among the Indians there. Discouragement and frustration inevitably set in, as his vision for reaching the Quichuas, and eventually the Aucas, sometimes took a back seat to nitty-gritty details of chores, construction, and labor relations. At one point Jim wrote in his journal:

How long, Lord, before they understand? Preaching, teaching, and having school all seem vain now as things move so slowly in the Indians' soul. Most of the young men are gone to the coast to work, including our most encouraging believers. God spare them the ravages of civilization and bring them back better men. . . . Lift up my soul, O Lord, for I am cast down. We want to see the Gospel spread, but how can it except it first take root in all the culture—old as well as young, men as well as women? . . . But, Lord, is this why we have trained them that they should leave the forest for white man's culture? Was it not that they should go reaching their own people with the Word? Wherein have we missed in setting before them the wrong ideal that they should regard money as of more worth to seek after than souls? Lead us out of it, Lord, and back to a simple principle of operation. School is a chore, house building, a heaviness now as I see little of what I aimed at accomplished.[1]

There were few entries in Pete's diary during the six months before he came home, probably because he was writing to me more often and making plans for us. Just before Jim's father arrived in April, Pete had experienced another bout with malaria, but a quick recovery had given him hope that his health was improving. A Quichua conference at another station had proved fruitful. The open conversions, the happiness of the believers and the nine who were baptized had clearly shown him that God's Spirit was working among those people. His diary entries convey a sense of fulfillment in the growth of the Quichua work, the traveling into unreached areas, and the new plans for contacting the Aucas. Leaving the others to finish the construction at Shandia, Pete returned to the States for our wedding.

16
UNITED

*H*aving completed the medical missions program at Biola, I returned to Seattle to prepare for the wedding. I looked forward to Pete's arrival, but not without some anxiety. How had we changed after two-and-a-half years? Once we spent time together, would we recognize that we had grown closer, or would we feel like we belonged in two different worlds? He was scheduled to arrive during the first week of June, 1954. We would have three weeks to get reacquainted and to work out past hurts before the wedding.

After all the waiting, however, I was unable to meet him at the airport. I had accepted a speaking engagement in Canada before I knew his arrival date and could not cancel. Though even this short delay frustrated me, Pete was understanding. What was one more day after all this time?

Actually, the extra day worked to our benefit. Instead of meeting Pete at the airport with all of his family around, he met me at the train station, alone, when I returned from Canada.

As my train slowly pulled into the station, I saw him standing by himself on the platform, earnestly searching the train windows. To my relief, he looked fit and healthy; I had worried that he would appear thin and sickly from his bouts with malaria. Excitedly I waved and knocked on my window, trying to get his attention. When he spotted me, he broke out into a shy smile and waved back. My heart raced. I had waited so long for this moment. What do I say? Where do we begin? Will we be like strangers?

I stepped off the train and right into Pete's open arms. For the first time in nearly three years, he held me and kissed me, just as he had done in the mountains that fateful weekend before Jim had shown up at his house. Now, the pain of those six months of turmoil and two-and-a-half years more of waiting quickly faded. Nothing mattered except the two of us. Over and over again, we said "I love you," "sweetheart," and "I missed you" to each other. We didn't lack for words. I was so grateful that we were alone.

Pete's father had loaned him the car so we could spend the afternoon together. Free to go where we wanted and return home when we wanted, we relished what turned out to be one of our few leisurely days before the wedding. The time apart, we realized, had brought much healing and growth, in our lives (especially in mine) and even in our parents'. My parents welcomed Pete warmly. By now they had given their blessing to our forthcoming marriage and our plans to return to Ecuador. While I had been finishing up at Biola, they had even made all the wedding arrangements. Likewise, Pete's father loved having Pete home and was glad we were getting married. (I had spent a lot of time with his dad and stepmother, Nellie, while Pete was away; we had become good friends.) He also seemed to be more accepting of Pete's initial decision to go to Ecuador.

We were married on June 26, 1954, in a Presbyterian church on Queen Ann Hill, close to Pete's home. I wore a beautiful borrowed wedding gown; Pete, a rented black suit and bowtie. More than two hundred guests attended the traditional ceremony. For the reception, my father's bakery gave us an elegant cake with pink flowers—a rarity for wedding cakes in those days. Some of our gifts stood out as well—a shotgun, for example. (Pete had circulated a list of items still needed for the jungle—not exactly your average bride's wish list!) It was a happy wedding, and Pete was ecstatic. Thankfully, we heard nothing of the criticisms leveled earlier about Pete's coming home.

We spent our honeymoon in a little cottage on Vancouver Island, where we relaxed, enjoyed the scenery, and played golf together. We also took some time to visit his mother's family, who lived on the island. Everyone has an embarrassing honeymoon moment to report. Mine was when I "sinned" with Pete and went to my very first Hollywood movie. Somehow I never dreamed I'd break this age-old family rule with a missionary. Pete's awkward moment was even better. He must have tried to act like Joe Cool when he made the reservations for our lodging, not letting on that it would be our honeymoon. When we arrived and he opened the door of our "honeymoon cottage," his face turned red and he fell silent. There, at the far end of the large room, stood two single beds. (He quickly took care of the situation.)

Speaking engagements, visiting old friends, and taking a trip down the Oregon coast with Pete's parents made the summer pass quickly. Pete's only diary entry for that summer speaks not of our wedding or our honeymoon, but of a boat trip with my Uncle John on Howe Sound (near Vancouver). I remember watching Pete standing at the bow, deep in thought, taking in the grandeur of God's creation. In his diary he wrote:

> With exhilarating speed on the water, the wind cold and salty on the face, the ready stance in the front of the boat as we took the swells and slapped down into the troughs of the waves. Closing my eyes, I could feel my body become one with the motion of the boat rolling with its

lurches and absorbing its shocks. My hands on the gunnel could feel the windshield stabbing sharply at my chin as we spanked the water and sent sheets out under the wide flair.—Howe Sound is beautiful with the mountains coming right down into the clear blue water and with the dark green and weathered grey of the rocky islands. It was a lovely outing.

I noted out in the rough that the swells and waves do not come in the measured pattern of waves breaking on the shore but in a mixed-up, turbulent, slanting series which throws the boat every which way—not a steady roll but a lurching to every side all at once. I also noted how the turbulence affected our little boat while the Black Ball Ferry moved without a trace of sway or motion. The closer we are to the upset the more we are affected. Many Christians [are] like the ferry—high and aloof off the water, not feeling the every movement [or] shock.

What he meant by this statement, I believe, is that many Christians set lofty ministry goals for themselves, but sometimes forget the needs of those they minister to. Unswerving commitment to the overall "work" is important, but the real work is caring for ordinary people and helping them. (Though Pete didn't mention it in his diary, after thinking these grand thoughts, he got seasick.)

As we prepared for our trip to South America, Pete decided to cancel my language study in Costa Rica. This surprised me, because he had felt so strongly that Costa Rica would be the best place for me to learn Spanish. His view hadn't changed, but other developments led him to feel that the wisest choice for us would be to head straight for Ecuador. First, there was a guest house available in Quito, recently rented for the Brethren missionaries to stay in whenever they came to town. A single woman missionary and a maid, Lucrecia, a

Quichua Indian, lived there, with plenty of room to spare. It seemed ideal: I would have no responsibility for the house and could spend all my time in language study. Pete also sensed Jim's discouragement with the construction and day-to-day tedium in the jungles, and felt it would slow operations if he stayed away another six months. In Quito, he reasoned, he could still fly to Shandia to help when needed, could save time for the Elliots and the McCullys by shopping for their supplies, and could continue his work on Quichua translation.

In September, we left Seattle by train for Los Angeles, having speaking engagements along the way. From Los Angeles we flew to Panama, where we boarded a ship for Ecuador, along with our barrels of wedding gifts and supplies. Those few days on the boat gave us much-needed rest and time alone. (We had lived either with his parents or mine all summer.) Pete had hoped that the boat's various stops would provide a gradual introduction to my new way of life, as it had for him. Unfortunately, we made only one port stop—Buenaventura, the city Pete had formerly described as a "hole." This time we avoided the meat market.

Nevertheless, the awful sights and smells bombarded my senses. *How could people live in such squalor?* I wondered. The green slime on the streets, the heat and humidity intensifying the smell, and the dirty, sickly children crying after us for money dramatized the depth of the people's physical and spiritual need. It seemed so incredibly hopeless. Buenaventura had *not* been a gentle introduction. The harsh reality of our mission, combined with the rough seas we encountered the next day, made me ill.

The muddy, debris-filled Guayas River leading to Ecuador's port city of Guayaquil did little to help me feel better. I was excited to reach Ecuador at last, but I also worried that I'd have trouble adjusting to our new life. No one met us in Guayaquil, because Pete now knew his way around. Even with the heat, humidity, undrinkable water, and bugs, the city was much nicer than Buenaventura. Pete made sure to book a better hotel than he and Jim had stayed in, however.

The second night we stayed in the Gospel Missionary Union house in Guayaquil—the first mission home I'd seen. The kind, caring spirit of the young family there helped me survive those early days of excitement, fear, nauseating smells, and strange food. They lived simply, but shared with us what they had, including boiled drinking water. Pete had succeeded in making my adjustment to that new country as easy as possible.

The flight from Guayaquil to Quito offered one breathtaking view after another, from the lush green jungle foliage to the high Andean snow-capped peaks and finally to Quito, nestled in the high plateau between the ranges. In contrast to the two port cities I had seen, Quito had beautiful surroundings, little heat, and no humidity. The sun shone warmly during the day, but our house remained cool, especially at night. I quickly discovered the energy-sapping ability of thin air at 9000 feet, but with no household duties, I considered it a great place to live and learn Spanish.

Within a few weeks of our arrival, however, circumstances changed to much less than ideal. The single woman, who had overseen the house affairs and served as a host for guests, left unexpectedly for the States because of a health problem. Suddenly Pete and I had to manage a guest house and a live-in maid, Lucrecia. Remembering his earlier conclusion that maids were unnecessary, Pete struggled as he tried to decide what to do with Lucrecia. He wanted our life to be simple and frugal, yet he also recognized that this young Indian woman needed a job and a place to live. And I needed to study Spanish. After prayer and deliberation, he realized she had to stay. I would never have managed without her help in the months that followed.

Running any house in a foreign country would be difficult, but a guest house was even more so. In those early days I could not communicate with Lucrecia at all, so Pete would tell her in Quichua what I wanted. Everything was strange for me. The tiny kitchen—even smaller than the bathroom—appeared to be the least important room in the house. On a good day it took hours to prepare meals in a country where the water and milk always had to be boiled, and where the high altitude lengthened cooking times. Since we had no refrigerator, I had to shop for food almost every day, giving up still more language study time. I seldom heard Spanish, because most of the house guests spoke English. Discouragement set in, just as it had for Pete when he first lived in Quito. We came here for one reason, I thought: to learn Spanish. Now it would take much longer than we had anticipated. How could we have made the mistake of not following our original plan to go to Costa Rica? Did we miss God's leading in coming to the house, or did God want us to learn something else here besides Spanish?

To make matters worse, I took sick again. Was the altitude affecting me, or was I just not coping well with all the changes? I wondered. Never before had I felt so weak and dehydrated. With the help of missionary doctors and nurses, I managed to get back on my feet. Pete and I dismissed the sickness, and moved ahead with our plan to visit the jungles in spite of the doctor's warning that I was too weak. Pete felt certain that my strength would improve once I left the high altitude.

We still had to decide the best way to get to the jungles. The tortuous, poorly maintained mountain roads made driving difficult, while the flight by the commercial airlines was equally hazardous. With the load of supplies we had for the jungle workers, and because of my recent illness, it was decided that we go by car—a much safer and more reliable means than by an Ecuadorian bus. Dr. Tidmarsh agreed to drive.

On the easiest part of the road, we encountered no problems. But our travel came to an abrupt halt where two mountain rivers joined in their descent to the jungles. A heavy downpour had washed away the bridge. As I gazed across the river, wondering what we would do, I noticed a crude wooden platform hanging from a heavy cable suspended high across the river where the bridge had been. The platform (called a *tarabita*), loaded with boxes and people, was precariously pulled across to the other side. One look at the platform and the river below, and I was ready to go back to Quito. But we piled the supplies on the platform, said good-bye to Dr. Tidmarsh, and climbed on ourselves. Somehow we made it.

On the other side, a typical Ecuadorian bus was filling up with people, bags, boxes, and chickens. We added our supplies to the load and hopped on. The bus clanked, bumped, and teetered down the mountains on a winding mud road barely the width of the bus—a road often closed due to mud slides. I tried to enjoy the beauty of the changing foliage as we descended from the higher elevations, to the tropical forest, where orchids covered the mountainside, but I couldn't forget the sheer drop on the other side of the bus. We appeared to be hanging over the edge of a precipice, with no guardrails. Surely a weight shift on the bus would send us over.

Eventually we arrived at the Mission Aviation Fellowship house in Shell Mera, much to my relief. The warm hospitality of pilot Nate Saint, and his wife, Marj, nearly caused me to forget the harrowing mountain trip (at least until our return to Quito).

From the descriptions Pete had given in his letters, I had thought I could picture what the flight into the jungles would look like, but the actual experience defied all imagining: a vast, deep-green carpet of dense rain forest, broken only by snaking rivers of brown. In the distance, Pete pointed to a small break in the trees: Shandia. Dropping the plane down over the Napo River for his final approach, Nate landed on the grassy airstrip, which stretched from the edge of the cliff (huge parts of which had fallen in the river during the flood) to a small stream several hundred yards back. Immediately several dozen Indians surrounded the plane, followed by the McCullys and the Elliots, who offered warm greetings. The day I had anticipated for so long had finally come. I felt like I was dreaming.

The Indians, overjoyed to have Pete back and curious about his bride, hovered around us and watched our every move, talking and laughing, scratching and slapping to keep the bugs away. I wondered if I would ever understand them or get used to the lack of privacy. Pete, on the other hand, enjoyed every minute of it; he felt at home.

The men had a lot of catching up to do, so they talked and laughed far into the night. Meanwhile, I had gone to bed because I wasn't feeling well. Severe cramps and abnormal bleeding told me something was wrong, but since I didn't want to spoil Pete's excitement, I told him not to worry. The next day I felt fine, and from then on I enjoyed my new experience in the jungles. By the time we returned to Quito, I had put the episode out of my mind.

In December, Pete and I prepared for our first Christmas together. The McCullys, who were expecting their second child, would be staying with us. Ed's parents would be visiting from the States as well. Everyone arrived amid much excitement, and on Christmas Eve we all went to bed, eagerly anticipating the events of the next day.

Late that night I was awakened by the same cramps I had experienced in Shandia, only this time I was hemorrhaging severely. Suddenly I realized—too late—what I had earlier suspected: I was pregnant and threatening to miscarry. Although we knew I needed medical attention, we hesitated to call the HCJB mission doctor, Paul Roberts, because it was so late on Christmas Eve. But as the hemorrhaging continued and I grew weaker, Pete finally called and I was rushed to the hospital.

My pregnancy caught Pete and me completely by surprise. When we got married, we had both decided not to start a family for at least two years. That way I could learn Spanish, get a good start on the Indian language, and settle into jungle living. My doctor in the States had told me I would have difficulty getting pregnant. When I had begun to feel nauseous on the boat, we chalked it up to seasickness. Then in Quito we assumed I had altitude sickness. With all the changes in my life and in the food I ate, there always seemed to be an explanation for my symptoms. Now we knew we had been mistaken.

I awoke on Christmas Day to the sun streaming through the window of a bare hospital room. I had no idea what time it was or what had happened to me. For what seemed like several hours, I saw no one. Where was Pete? Here I was, alone on Christmas Day in a hospital in a foreign country, with no way of contacting anyone. I realized that I must have miscarried, and wondered what might have happened to me if I had hemorrhaged in the jungles.

Eventually someone came, who I presumed was a nurse. Since I had not learned enough Spanish, however, I could not communicate with her. I didn't know what my condition was, how long I would be stuck in the hospital, when I could see a doctor. She said only one thing I understood: that I had to stay in bed. At this point the frustration was more than I could handle. I knew everyone was busy with Christmas, but I couldn't understand why Pete didn't stay with me. The unappetizing meal I received only reminded me of the Christmas turkey dinner I was missing with Pete and the McCullys. (The senior McCullys had brought the turkey with them from the States.) I cried the rest of the afternoon, feeling very sorry for myself. I had missed our first Christmas and lost our first baby, and I felt that Pete didn't care.

When Pete showed up at the end of the day to bring me home, I was angry and upset. It had never occurred to him that I needed him, he said. He was told that I would probably be asleep from the medication, and that the nurses would help if I needed anything. When he went on to tell me what we were given for Christmas and how good the dinner was, I felt even worse. He had been thoughtless to leave me alone in a strange place, I believed, especially during an emergency situation.

Dr. Roberts later explained to me that miscarriages were not unusual. Mine was more serious because I had hemorrhaged so much. I needed to accept it as God's will and for my best. Perhaps this was part of the sacrifice I had to make for missionary life, I thought. But at that moment, my noble ideal of "doing all things through Christ" came face to face with the cold reality of life: I felt completely dependent on Pete, a burden to him, and the very thing he had feared—a wife that would hinder his work for the Lord.

Once my strength returned, I had to act as hostess for a steady stream of visitors, which meant my language study suffered. My language teacher scolded me for my lack of progress, which only discouraged me further. Why wasn't I like Pete, Jim, and Betty, who were so good in the language? she would ask me. I felt like a failure, and began to question God's will in leading me to Ecuador. My slow progress was hampering Pete's ministry. Why did it seem that everything was going wrong? Pete tried to encourage me, but I only grew more depressed.

After one of my physical checkups, Dr. Roberts and his wife invited us to their home. That night they talked to us as friends, sharing from their own experience. They helped me understand that my miscarriage had taken its toll on me physically and emotionally, and that Pete and I needed to talk about it. (We hadn't.) The doctor gently reminded Pete that he was no longer single and had to think about his wife. We were experiencing the real stuff of married life, he said, with real pain and real feelings that we needed to deal with together. Healing would not come merely by saying everything was God's will.

That conversation with them marked a turning point in my relationship with Pete. We began to talk more openly with each other, and share more of our feelings. Pete also let me read his diaries for the first time.

Up to that point I had felt Pete could not understand my overwhelming feelings of depression and failure. But when I started to read his diary, I saw—to my surprise—all the very same feelings: his own discouragement in learning the language, his awful struggles with depression when he had malaria, his frustration over his lack of practical skills, the doubts about his usefulness on the field. He too had felt he was letting everyone down during his illnesses. He had never shared these feelings with me in his letters. I had viewed him as strong, competent, trusting the Lord with an unshakable faith. Apparently, that was what he had wanted me and others to believe. He kept his weaknesses and his struggles to himself, expressing them only in his diary. As I read about all those feelings and talked with Pete about them, I came to understand him in a much deeper way. And as I reminded him of his past struggles, he found it easier to understand mine. We tried to step down from the unrealistic, "spiritual" plane of living where only "the work" mattered, and started to share our feelings honestly with each other.

Toward the end of our time in Quito, a young Christian couple entered our lives. The husband, a student at the university in Quito, felt his courses were undermining his faith. Someone had recommended that he go to Pete for help. Pete's time with this young man reawakened his initial desire to minister on a college campus. He had felt that yearning earlier, shortly after his arrival in Ecuador. He had then written in his diary about his desire "to meet head on the college mind, intelligently and with a full knowledge of God and his presence to keep the work from being dry and brittle. These months away from university life have given me what I had only in theory . . . in the university: full confidence in God and that he has done *all things well.*"

Now, a new idea crossed his mind. No one was currently working with university students in Quito. With his Master's degree in American literature, he could teach on campus and organize a student Christian fellowship. Some of the older missionaries had encouraged him to consider this ministry. Together Pete and I considered spending just a few more years in the jungle work, and then returning to Quito, where he would teach. He knew his health had suffered in the jungles, and didn't expect to last much longer there. But he wanted to follow through on his commitment to Jim and Ed until these crucial pioneering years were over.

While I finished up my Spanish lessons, Pete worked on Bible translation and periodically visited nearby missions to teach the Scriptures to the mountain Quichua Indians. Thousands of these Indians lived in the vicinity, but very few missionaries knew the language well enough to teach them from the Bible. In the summer of 1955, Pete took me down the western side of the Andes to see the work of fellow missionaries among the Spanish-speaking whites and the Colorado Indians. Pete taught in the Spanish church, and we witnessed the birth of a church among the Colorados.

Before leaving for the jungles, we had to move from the large house to a small apartment, prepare for the first retreat of all the Brethren missionaries, and cope with more illness. This time I felt sure I was pregnant again, and went straight to the doctor. He ordered immediate bed rest, but I didn't get much, since I needed to ready the apartment for our fellow workers. The fear of another miscarriage haunted me. Sure enough, the night before the retreat, I threatened to miscarry again. The next morning Pete and the others left for the retreat, and I stayed with a missionary family at HCJB. Once again I spent several difficult days alone in bed, wondering why God allowed these things to happen, and always at the wrong time.

When Pete came back after the retreat, we stayed together at the house of another HCJB doctor, Art Johnston, hoping to prevent the miscarriage. But it happened anyway, and I had to stay in the hospital again. This experience, painful as it was, stood in sharp contrast to my previous hospital visit. Pete lovingly cared for me during my entire stay, listening to my sadness and frustration and sharing his own. The healing and growth in our relationship had truly begun.

I still felt badly for him, however, because again I had delayed his plans to return to the jungles. We couldn't wait much longer, as Pete was scheduled to teach at the first short-term Quichua Bible school at Dos Rios. In August, once I regained some of my strength, we flew from Quito to Shell Mera rather than travel on the roads. The Saint home in Shell Mera provided a good place for me to recuperate for a few days before flying to the jungle station at Dos Rios. Soon I would be living in the jungles. But I recalled at one point how I had joked with a friend in the States with the comment, "They'll probably find those elusive Aucas after I get to the jungles!"

17
AUCAS FOUND

*F*rom Shell Mera we flew back to Shandia in September 1955. We would stay only for a few days before going to a mission station in Dos Rios, where Pete and Jim would conduct a three-week "Bible Institute" for the Quichuas. Then we would move to Puyupungu to continue the Quichua work Jim and Betty had started.

After a fifteen-month absence from Shandia, Pete noted that the Indians were "more effusive than ever in their welcome." They begged us to stay. To Pete it seemed "kind of unfair to dash right off again to Dos Rios," and then have to tell the Indians we were moving to Puyupungu for some months. But "it couldn't be helped," he wrote, because he felt committed to the new work at Puyupungu. As we prepared to leave, "They all gathered after the service on Sunday & begged us to stay—one after the other or all together & it was quite a scene. It was a great joy to see the many new converts & to see the happiness on their faces."

The Dos Rios institute was a first among the Quichuas. Thirteen Indians came, two of them young women. Pete taught from the book of James; Jim, Bible Synopsis and History; and two nationals taught Basic Doctrines and Personal Evangelism. Pete wrote:

> In my class on the book of James, I am having each of the students give a little exposition to the rest on some selected passage. Yesterday Santiago Calapucha spoke excellently on the "prayer of faith" from chapter 5. I had given him only the sketchiest outline and he developed it himself bringing in Peter's sinking in the water and ending with an exhortation to stir us up to more believing prayer. It was the first message in Quichua I have ever heard on believing prayer and even the first time I had ever heard the idea developed by an Indian believer—what an encouragement. It shows how necessary book by book exposition of the Scriptures is and how it develops and broadens the Indians' spiritual life.

The practical teaching of James easily applied to the Indians' own situation. Pete spoke on

> "filthy talk" and our responsibility to put away all kinds of filthiness. . . . The boys immediately were really earnest and attentive and admitted the vastness of the problem. They pointed out how universal it is and how difficult it is to get away from it but resolved to do everything in their power to put an end to it in their lives.

Watching the Indians learn renewed Pete's enthusiasm and vision for the Quichua work. He realized that the Indians could be trained as teachers and itinerant evangelists among their own people, and adopted this approach in his work with them, developing and leading intense short-term workshops he called "Bible institutes."

Three weeks in Dos Rios gave me plenty of time to learn more about jungle living. I helped the missionary wife there bake bread, and learned how to cook manioc root and bananas.

One of the women students, Fanny, spoke fluent Spanish and during her free periods spent time with me. I enjoyed practicing my Spanish with her, and picked up a little Quichua as well. I also taught her to swim, an activity the women seldom learned. Usually the men were taught to swim as boys in order to spear fish at the bottom of the river. Swimming was how we cooled off, bathed, and washed our hair.

On the last Sunday of the institute, the students were sent out as evangelists to their people. They were split up into four groups, each accompanied by a missionary or teacher, and assigned to different areas. Pete and I, along with Morrie Fuller, the Alliance missionary at Dos Rios, ventured with one group of Indians into an area never before visited by missionaries. The day before we had secured permission from the Indians' owner to visit, and we had hired horses for the trip. Early on Sunday morning, however, when we went to pick up the horses, they were suddenly unavailable. We suspected that someone was trying to stop us, but decided simply to walk into the area. Interestingly, we had not walked far when a horseman passed us in a great hurry.

When we finally reached the Indian village, no one was in sight. Piecing together the morning's events, we concluded that because the lack of horses had not deterred us, the horseman was sent to warn the Indians of our coming. We waited for a while in the clearing, watching for some sign of life. Soon a few children popped their heads from behind the trees. Pete and Morrie pulled out a collection of trinkets they had brought, and before long a number of children had gathered around us. Several women also appeared, murmuring among themselves, but they did not come near us for almost an hour. Then, one by one, they came up to us, shook hands, and officially welcomed us to their village.

We sang Quichua Christian songs, after which the Christian Indians presented a simple gospel message to the women and children. We learned later why the women had welcomed us: One of them had recognized Morrie from another station where she had lived as a young girl years before. Although Morrie could not speak Quichua, he had evidently communicated what was really important, for she called him a "lover of Indians." Unfortunately, the men of the village had all left; we wondered if our visit had prompted the owner to send them off to work.

While Jim and Pete were teaching at the institute, Ed and Nate took a casual flight over the northern edge of the Auca territory. Visibility happened to be especially good that day, and Nate thought it a perfect opportunity to explore. Little did they know what they'd find that day. Nate wrote in his journal:

> We followed the Nushino east, but flying the north side this time. We were able to scan a six- or eight-mile swath. About fifty miles east of Ed's place [Arajuno], out over the middle of nowhere, we turned due north toward Coca on the Rio Napo. About five minutes later we spied some spots that looked as if they might have been planted manioc patches years ago. It's hard to be sure from a bird's point of view, even after you've been studying the woods for some time. We circled and then went on north until the Napo was getting close, without seeing anything more. The left turn toward home was inevitable. We didn't have gas enough to press on much farther and we had covered what we had outlined for this particular trip. However, it was hard to give up. It takes so long to get that far out, and it is so difficult to find such ideal weather. I'd been eyeing a blemish, barely discernible in the jungle, maybe five miles away. Ed couldn't make it out, but we decided to fly that way for just a couple of minutes, and if we didn't turn up something more concrete we'd beat it for home.

The blemish grew into a well-defined pockmark, and then into a good-sized clearing covered with well-cleaned manioc. *This was it.* We'd been cruising very slowly and our fuel consumption was getting low, but we could still hang around for fifteen minutes without cutting into the reserve. So we hung around. All told, we must have seen about fifteen clearings and a few houses. It was an exciting old time . . . a time we'd waited for.[1]

The missionaries had spotted Auca houses for the first time.

Following the institute, I flew with Pete to Arajuno, where the McCullys lived. I would stay there with Marilou while Nate shuttled Ed, Pete, and Jim to several unevangelized Quichua settlements near the jungle town of Villano. Nate and Ed took advantage of the opportunity to fill in Pete and Jim about their exciting new discoveries, as they had agreed to keep their Auca discussions secret and off the radio.

The flights to Villano took the men directly over Auca territory. Nate had taken a different route each time to survey the area. Shortly after leaving on one flight with Pete, the men saw something.

"About fifteen minutes from Arajuno we spotted some clearings," Nate wrote. ". . . We flew down a little river and spotted a half-dozen big houses with smaller ones around them. That was it. There they were as plain as the nose on your face *and only fifteen minutes from Ed's place at Arajuno by plane.*"[2]

When they returned to Arajuno they could hardly contain their excitement. At last they had found the Aucas, whom they had prayed for and sought for so long. And they were practically in Ed's back yard. Pete's reaction in his diary:

I had the thrill of seeing my first Auca houses. . . . we saw several large houses and a number of smaller ones along the banks of the river. This gave us a real spurt toward making some plans for the Aucas. We concluded that we ought to begin immediately making frequent visits to them dropping presents—Nate is busy perfecting his bucket drop. . . . Jim and Betty are going to see if we can get some linguistic material from Rachel [Saint] for we all feel that we must begin bit by bit to lay a basis for future contact with them.

They had found the Aucas—and I had only been in the jungles for one month. At first I was excited for the men. But then an entry I had read in Pete's diary (when he had asked me to marry him) came to mind: "I feel that if pushed to it, Olive would rather have me die after we had lived together than to indefinitely postpone our wedding in the possibility that something fatal might happen." His words seemed rather ominous in light of this new discovery, and my excitement cooled.

While the other men shifted their attention to the Aucas, Pete and I prepared to leave for Puyupungu. We would travel by canoe, and our wedding gifts and supplies, which had been stored at Shandia for the past year, would be flown in once we cleared the overgrown airstrip. After months of expectation and prayer, we finally left for our new jungle home and ministry. Pete, however, was feeling torn between the work at Puyupungu and the chance to reach the Aucas.

On October 17, at Puyu, a small town down the road from Shell Mera, we climbed into one of several dugout canoes bound for Puyupungu. Jim, Ed, and Pete had canoed down this river on their big survey trip two years earlier. Pete wrote in his diary that this trip "was as exciting as before—not hazardous as I had remembered it but thrilling in spots." Traveling by canoe allowed Pete to visit all the Indian houses along the Puyu River and tell them about the school at Puyupungu. We had also sent word to the Puyupungu Indians that we would be coming.

A far cry from the relaxing canoe jaunts Pete and I used to take in Seattle, I enjoyed my first jungle canoe ride to the fullest—if screaming is any measure of enjoyment. The Indians, using long poles, skillfully maneuvered the canoes around fallen trees, over rocks in the shallow areas, and between huge boulders as we plunged through troughs of fast water. I found it as exhilarating as a roller coaster, though far more dangerous. Because of less-than-usual rainfall over the past month, the river was quite low, forcing us to get out in places while the Indians carried the canoes over rocks. Once out of the white water, we moved peacefully downriver. Just before the Puyu joined the larger Pastaza River, we pulled to the side and climbed the riverbank. From there I could see our new home.

Pete described the area and its people in a letter to friends:

Puyupungu is a lovely spot on a high bank overlooking one of the huge thundering tributaries of the Amazon with the whole eastern range of the Andes looming up in front of us. It is a gorgeous place but is a good example of the description of mankind found in Romans 1. For the people here have been living for centuries without the knowledge of Christ and have been enslaved by the drunken babblings of witchdoctors who determine the beliefs of the tribe while in a stupor caused by drinking a wild herb. Such utterances, given by the man while apparently unconscious and prompted by Satanic forces, have been the basis for superstitions and practices for centuries.

Our first days in Puyupungu were "primitive," according to Pete. If *he* thought they were primitive, I felt they were all that and more. "Olive struggled with cooking in just one or two pots, with two tin plates, one knife, fork and spoon and other small inconveniences," he wrote. "Only one air mattress and one blanket made sleeping a problem. The Indians had cleaned the airstrip for us as well as the plaza. . . . the plane has come in several times bringing loads of equipment."

In the same diary entry, Pete abruptly switched to the other subject on his mind:

> The finding of the Auca houses has spurred us on to real activity with Nate and Ed doing most of the thinking and planning while Jim and I are helping financially and by prayer at present. The day we left Arajuno, October 6, was an important day in Auca work—the first contact by air was made in a flight drop, dropping by "the bucket" method, a brightly decorated aluminum pot. . . . They saw no one but saw many evidences of life. . . . Last week a return trip was made and a notable advance in relations was seen. . . . We are walking gradually into more and more contact with them and must be ready for anything.

Though his thoughts never strayed far from the Aucas, Pete concentrated on the work in Puyupungu. He was disappointed to find that some of the key Indian men he had planned to work with had left for the coasts, or for jungle labor jobs, in search of the white man's money. Pete had hoped to teach these particular Indians to read and then to study the Scriptures. But he had long since learned to expect interruptions like these and to work with the changes, so he began his plans for a big Christmas fiesta, which would bring all the Indians together for a good time of eating, playing, and learning the Bible. Ed and Jim had agreed to come and teach.

By the first of November, Pete wrote that our life had settled down to normal. I had successfully baked cookies and my first loaf of bread on the small wood stove. The Indians especially loved bread-baking days, and the good smells always brought them to the door for a piece. Our little gas refrigerator fascinated them: How could a little hot flame on the outside of the box make the inside so cold? Holding an ice cube was a frightening new experience for them—so cold in their hand that it hurt. Pete pointed above the trees to the snow-capped mountain peaks, and tried to explain that the snow on those mountains was cold just like that ice.

As we suffered in the humid jungle heat, I often gazed at those magnificent Andes, marveling that they were so close and yet so cool. One mountain, Sangay, was not only snow-capped, but also an active volcano. After watching it spew one day, Pete wrote:

> Sangay just put on a spectacular display for us—all the more thrilling with the binoculars [a wedding gift]. At night it looks like a huge bonfire out of which shoot flares in a long graceful arc landing a couple thousand feet down the mountainside. With the binoculars we could see individual balls of fire burst and spray out all over. It was a real show and clouds of steam coming from the lava on the snow would momentarily blot out the 4th of July fireworks display, only to have it clear and start over again.

I suppose some of my friends and family back in the States considered me brave and fearless when I left for the wild jungles. I only wish I had been more so. Many aspects of jungle living left me scared and squeamish. Our house, for instance, which Jim had built, stood on stilts about nine feet off the ground, and had a quaint grass roof. I liked the roof until I discovered that it accommodated spiders and scorpions which sometimes dropped into the house. At night the cockroaches moved in, only to be driven out briefly by an invasion of army ants.

One night I learned not to store our baskets of food supplies under the house, even though hanging high up on the posts. A terrible commotion under the floor awakened us.

Fearing that we'd lose our food, I jumped up and ran outside with a flashlight, only to find myself looking into the big eyes and soft noses of the Indian chief's cows. I let Pete chase them away.

I always looked carefully before reaching into the wood pile after I once found a tarantula there. To help me recognize poisonous snakes, Pete told the Indians to bring me some they had killed. (I really didn't think it was necessary.) When someone found a snake hanging around a pineapple, I decided to leave pineapple-cutting to the Indians. The Saints gave us one of their dogs, partly for company but mostly to scare away all the snakes. And Pete wrote that our life was back to normal!

While he got the school in order, supervised the teaching of the school children, and taught the Indians on Sunday, I took over the medical side of the work and struggled to learn Quichua. In order to treat the Indians, I often had to write down what I heard and then find Pete in order to determine the diagnosis. I assisted in delivering two babies soon after we arrived. It frightened me to handle a birth on my own, but I thanked the Lord that all went well and that the babies arrived safely. At times I saw how our gift of medicine broke down barriers of fear between us and the Indians from other areas. When they got sick, they came to us for help, and in turn heard God's Word.

Seventeen students attended the school, with a young Christian Quichua teacher from Shandia in charge. But more Indian children from further upriver would attend if they had a place to stay. The question of building a dormitory arose. The Indians looked to Pete for an answer, expecting him to tell them what to do. Pete, however, wanted to train the Indians to make their own decisions about running the school. Somehow he needed to teach them to take responsibility without ordering them around. He had an idea. One day he called the Indians together and suggested that they form a "Padres de Familia"—

that is, a PTA. Then they held an election to choose a president and a secretary, something they had never done. One by one, they whispered their choices to Pete with great enthusiasm.

With a board of responsible Indians now in place, Pete discussed with them the need for a school dormitory and the idea of having a Christmas fiesta. Preparing for a fiesta so excited the Indians that they wanted to put off the dormitory until afterward; Pete gently helped them to establish their priorities. To the Indians, a typical fiesta meant little other than eating, drinking, and merriment. Pete had something different in mind. He explained to the Indians that this fiesta would have lots of food and fun, but also would include Bible teaching. And no alcohol would be permitted. The Indians couldn't imagine a fiesta without alcohol, and felt its absence would bother the Indians from other villages. But Pete stood his ground and told them it was absolutely prohibited. Reluctantly they consented.

Building the school dormitory and preparing for the fiesta energized the Indians. Everyone had a job to do. And all of the activity brought more Indians to the Sunday meetings, where Pete taught them about God and how Christ had died for them. One day a young Indian man told Pete that he now believed in Christ—the first visible sign of God's moving among the people.

Two weeks later Pete wrote,

Today the angels are rejoicing over Puyupungu and so are we! How faithful God is! This morning a number of Indians decided for Christ. I felt led to speak on baptism since I had noted several misunderstandings while I listened to Indians talk. So after speaking from the story of Philip and the eunuch, I tried to explain simply and clearly the difference between faith and baptism. After an early fight with squalling babies the attention was excellent and I felt the Spirit moving in hearts, so asked for a show of hands after carefully explaining what a decision for Christ would involve. A number of hands showed up—Tito, Benito, Pascual, and others. A number more began to put up their hands when Alejo broke out from the back telling them that it would mean giving up drinking and living immorally. Some of the hands went down at that. I closed in prayer, inviting those who were really repentant to go into the back room of the school where I could deal more carefully with them. Twelve came. . . . We encouraged and exhorted them and arranged for a believers' meeting on Friday afternoon. Several others are very close. . . . and our heart is still burdened for the Chief Atanacio, who hasn't decided yet—but what joy, this is what we came here for.

On his twenty-seventh birthday, Pete wrote, "How good God has been and how full and blessed His ways. How continually I thank God for bringing me here almost overcoming the impossible and pushing me out—I felt 'thrust out' and how grateful I am for God's impelling."

In November, amid preparation for the fiesta, a Wycliffe Bible translator by the name of Betsy joined us for several weeks to work on the Quichua language. She asked for Pete's help and wanted to check her dictionary against his. But her presence highlighted the issue missionaries face when reducing a language to writing and translating. There are different methods. What symbols does one use for the sounds? Disagreement can easily arise over this issue.

The issue of which translation method to use affected me, too, as I was struggling to learn Quichua at that time. Two different phonetic systems were in use—the linguistic one of Wycliffe and the use of ordinary letters as pronounced in Spanish. The missionaries had sharp differences over which was best. Jim and Betty were using the Wycliffe method, setting down the unwritten Quichua language in linguistically "cor-rect" phonetics. But Dr. Tidmarsh had adopted the Spanish letters because he knew that eventually the Quichuas would learn Spanish. It seemed more sensible and easier for the Indians to learn just one set of phonetic symbols rather than two. Pete, who hadn't had linguistic training, used the method he learned from Jim and Betty. Later, however, he began to see the advantages for the Indians to learn the Spanish letters.

Nevertheless, I was caught between these theories. Betty's strong opinions about the subject made it even more difficult for me to know what to do. The issue was not only one of methodology, but of sensitivity to the Indians themselves. At about this time, Pete remarked to me how he was impressed that Betty's gifts tended more toward intellectual pursuits than to personal ministry. He actually began praying that God would lead her into a writing ministry.

Meanwhile, "Operation Auca" was moving ahead. Nate and Ed had been making weekly flights and bucket drops over the newly discovered Auca settlement from Arajuno, the nearest mission airstrip. (Jim, who stayed in Shandia with Betty, also went on several of the flights.) We received progress reports from Nate when he flew into Puyupungu each week bringing food and mail. As Pete heard all about the gifts passed back and forth, and the Aucas' apparent friendliness and enthusiasm, he regretted not being in Arajuno to participate.

Though Pete shared the excitement of the other men in their progress with the Aucas, he did not feel their same sense of urgency in establishing ground contact. Perhaps it was because he had not yet seen the Aucas himself; the others had. Plus, there was the upcoming fiesta at Puyupungu and the New Year's conference at Shandia to prepare for. Nevertheless, when the others suggested the first week of December as the date for a first attempt, he opposed the timing, and wrote a letter to them explaining why.

190

Betty later summed up the various views of the men in *Through Gates of Splendor*:

> Pete, who constantly conferred with the other three, did not feel that the next full moon [early December] was the right time for the first attempt at contact. It was too soon to assume that a long-standing hatred of white men had been overcome. The language problem was a big one— and it lay within their power to gain more knowledge of it, by working with Dayuma, the escaped Auca woman from whom Jim had gathered his material. Ed's reaction was that the next move should not necessarily be an effort at contact, but rather the establishment of a usable airstrip down the Curaray [River], perhaps within five miles of the "neighborhood" [of the Auca village]. Meanwhile Jim was "chewing the bit." If a friendly contact were made, Jim and I were prepared to leave the work in Shandia for a time, and go in and live among the Aucas. Nate felt that the men should follow the already-established course of making regular contacts and that nothing should be done suddenly, but that each advance be allowed to "soak in" before pressing another.[3]

"The team has a spectrum that ranges from impatience to conservatism," Nate wrote. Pete was the conservative; Jim, the impatient one. The men finally agreed to delay ground contact until after the New Year.

On one of Nate's weekly visits to Puyupungu, he brought Roger Youderian, a missionary with Gospel Missionary Union, to meet us. We had never met, but we knew about his pioneering work among the Jivaro and the Atshuara Indians. Nate knew Roger well and believed his experience would be valuable for "Operation Auca."[4] That afternoon the three men talked about ways to reach the Aucas. They discussed several articles in *Brown Gold* magazine [from New Tribes mission] that gave an account of five men who were killed trying to reach an Indian tribe in Bolivia in 1943. Not wanting to repeat anyone's mistakes, Roger, Pete, and Nate tried to learn all they could from these reports. Pete liked having Roger involved; he felt they would all benefit from his expertise.

The flights continued through November and into December. Pete wrote:

> The Auca situation is developing fast. A definite attempt at contact is planned for early January. The attitude seems increasingly friendly as the weekly flights are made, gifts are returned, platforms are constructed to lead the "cheering section" [of curious Aucas], a model airplane has appeared on the roofs, no signs of hostility appear at all and on the other hand enthusiastic welcome is shown everywhere. All of this makes the guys feel that a trip should be made now as soon as the conferences are over, even though we don't have any more language info from Ila [where Dayuma was]. They feel the Ila situation is too touchy and too public for us to be able to get much info without jeopardizing the whole project. Perhaps so—I don't know it from close hand. There is to be a pow wow about it at Arajuno during Christmas. Ed, Jim and Roger are definitely going—either Nate or I might make up the other one.

Up to that point the plan had been to go by canoe, and room would be limited to four men and two Quichua guides. Pete hated to be so far from the action, and grieved over the possibility that he might not be able to go with the others.

The day of the Christmas fiesta finally arrived, and all plans for reaching the Aucas were set aside for a few days. Jim, Ed, and Pete turned their attention to nearly a hundred Indians who had come from all along the Puyu River to have fun and learn about the Bible. We considered it a great success. Only one "incident" occurred when several bottles of gin were discovered. Rather than dispose of the liquor, the men decided to return it to the offending Indian after the fiesta ended. "No one held a grudge against us," Pete later noted.

Midway through the fiesta, Nate flew in unexpectedly. Ed McCully's wife, Marilou, alone at Arajuno with their two small boys, had radioed an urgent message to Marj Saint at Shell Mera. A naked Auca Indian carrying a lance had been seen by a Quichua early that morning, barely fifty yards from their house. The Auca had fled, but a telltale footprint left no question that he had visited. Ed immediately jumped in the plane with Nate, and they rushed back to Arajuno. Nothing more was seen of the intruder, but the incident served to remind us that perhaps there was more to this seemingly friendly people than met the eye.

18
NIGHTMARE

*A*s the men continued their aerial gift drops over the Auca village, Nate noticed a number of sandbars along the Curaray River. Rainfall had been sparse during the past few months, resulting in abnormally low water levels. It occurred to him that he might find a beach long enough for a landing. After several more scouting flights, he located an ideal sandbar—long enough to land on and reasonably close to the Auca houses. Now the men could fly in, set up camp on "Palm Beach"— their nickname for the spot—and wait for a visit from the Aucas. Nate would fly in and out each day, allowing for an easy transfer of people, equipment, or supplies as needed. Both Nate and those on the beach would have radios to keep in touch with the rest of us. Everyone felt much more secure with this arrangement than with the more dangerous canoe trip through Auca country, which also would have isolated them from air access.

Once Nate found the beach, ground contact with the Aucas no longer remained an idealistic goal. It was a realistic, immediate possibility. The next full moon, their last chance for an attempt before the rains, would come within two weeks.

Pete and I now had to face the real issue of whether he would go. Up to this point, he had participated in most of the planning, but hadn't yet committed himself to be one of the actual members of the landing party. We needed to decide before we left Puyupungu for a December 23 planning meeting at Arajuno, where we would also celebrate Christmas.

"Pete, are you going to go?" I asked him directly, afraid that I already knew the answer. It had been four years and four months since he first told me that God had called him to the Aucas as a single man. That decision he had made without me. Now I was facing the very situation he had wanted to keep me from. That fatal diary entry, I realized, was almost a prediction. Yes, he could still go. And yes, I would rather have this short time with him than no time at all. But the danger was real. There was a cost to be counted, and now I was part of that cost. We had both prayed for the opportunity to reach the Aucas. But somehow I had expected God to make it easier.

"It's been on my mind a lot," Pete said, "but I have no clear answer. I'm not rugged like the others, and not as jungle-wise. I'm not sure what I can contribute to the team at this point. My presence might even hinder the expedition. I'm really torn between wanting to be part of the team and feeling responsible for the Quichua ministry here. And I have you to think about. You haven't been here long and so much has happened. Do I have the right to put you through this right now?"

"Honey, I don't want to keep you from going," I said, trying to be as honest as I could. The full impact of my words didn't register in my mind. I avoided thinking about death. I realized how much easier the decision would be if he had remained single. But now we believed that God had brought our lives together. We had to trust him. Surely he would not fail us. I felt very close to Pete as we earnestly prayed about what to do. We didn't come to an absolute decision before leaving Puyupungu, but I knew he wanted to go.

At the planning meeting in Arajuno, the men agreed that the time was right to move ahead. Although Roger and Barbara Youderian couldn't come, Roger had already laid out a plan for the operation. Safety was a priority. They would build a tree house for three men to sleep in, which offered greater protection from an ambush. Nate, rather than staying over-night, would fly in each morning and leave before dark, maintaining regular radio contact with Marj in Shell Mera from his plane. On the beach, the men would keep another radio. Then they discussed whether to take guns. Not knowing what wild animals they might encounter, they agreed to bring several pistols along. But the men vowed not to use them to spare their own lives. They would fire only to frighten the Aucas if that became necessary.

As the discussion progressed, Pete said very little. He realized that everyone's role was in place except for his. Jim, Ed, and Roger would stay in the tree house; Nate would fly them in. Pete wondered where he would fit in.

"What about you, Pete, are you going?" Ed finally asked.

Pete started to answer when Jim piped up. "I don't think it's wise to put all our eggs into one basket in case something happens. If Pete goes then we have the three Quichua-speaking men together in a dangerous situation. If anything happens, there goes the Quichua work." For once, Jim was showing caution and counting the cost. But I saw the dejected look on Pete's face.

Then Ed broke in. "Come on, Jim. What do you mean 'if anything happens'? Do you think I'd go if I thought we'd be killed? Look at Marilou. [She was pregnant.] I'm convinced that those Indians want to be friends. We have watched them and God has answered our prayers. Marilou and I and our two boys have lived here on Auca land for almost a year, and the

196

Aucas haven't done anything to us. And we know for sure they've been here. We are taking every precaution on this trip. We have the tree house and we're talking about taking guns. I think Pete should go if God is leading him. We could use more hands."

"Listen fellows," Nate said, "I sure could use some help on the flights. Pete could fly out to Palm Beach each day with me and then back to Arajuno each night." (Nate's diary shows he had pegged Pete for this role at least two weeks earlier. Pete was the lightest of the four men, making Nate's beach takeoffs and landings easier.) Pete brightened somewhat at this suggestion.

"I want to join you if I can be of help," Pete finally said. So they all agreed to include him. If all went according to schedule, the whole group would be on the beach by January 3.

Pete was in, though not without some trepidation. He wrote:

> It was decided that perhaps I ought to prepare to go on the expedition in order to gain by numbers more relative security for all. I am glad to go and when my heart begins to be troubled at all, the Lord has quieted me, once with calling my attention to the intricate care given to the forming of a toucan hung on the wall in the bathroom— "His eye is on the sparrow"—and once with [the passage] "Let not your heart be troubled neither let it be afraid."

Our first Christmas in the jungles was much happier for me than the previous Christmas in Quito. Yet the significance of the day went beyond the holiday celebration. It was a Sunday with the regular evangelistic service with the Quichua Indians, followed by the baptism of five new believers.

The afternoon of Christmas Day, the men returned to the subject on everyone's mind—the Aucas. They studied what they knew of the Auca language, practicing phrases on each other. At night, by the light of kerosene lanterns, we played games and laughed, trying not to think of the dangers ahead. During the next few days, Jim, Ed, and Pete busily prepared for Operation Auca, cutting wood for the tree house, gathering supplies, memorizing Auca phrases—all with an air of anticipation.

We left for the Quichua New Year's conference in Shandia the following day. One evening during the conference, Betty and I talked alone.

"So how do you feel about the men going to the Aucas?" she asked.

"Can't say that I'm very happy," I replied. "I feel very uneasy because who knows what can happen? Jim and Pete didn't spare us from the possible dangers while they were single, but I can't help but think about those days and the uncertain future I face, all because of the Aucas. What about you?"

"Jim and I talked about going down to the Aucas as a family. If he is going to die I would rather die with him."

"Yes, and the other fellows weren't very happy about that plan."

"Olive, what will you do if Pete is killed?"

Whatever would I do? I wondered. The real possibility of that outcome was only beginning to sink in.

"I would go home, I guess. I haven't wanted to think about it. What could I do alone here? I don't know the language. I imagine you would stay, right?"

"Yes."

The closer it got to January 2, when the men would assemble at Arajuno for their flight to Palm Beach, the more afraid I grew. My thoughts were filled with recollections of things I'd read in my anthropology course about certain hostile Indian tribes. Often the Indians would appear friendly, then without warning rise up and murder those who had befriended them. While I was at Biola, I had heard about two missionaries in New Guinea who were killed suddenly after apparently befriending the natives of a primitive tribe there. No one seemed to know what had happened. I worried that the same thing would happen with the Aucas. And I picked up a case of the flu.

On January 2, 1956, all five men were in Arajuno making the final preparations for the flights to Palm Beach the following day. Marilou, Barbara, and I were the only wives there. That day was the first time I had met Barbara. It helped me to see her happy spirit because I knew that she had already experienced having her husband walk into a dangerous situation, and alone at that.

That night, a few light moments interrupted the seriousness of the situation and my own uneasiness. Usually Ed and Jim provided the quick wit, but this time Pete took a turn. He read out loud from a letter he and I had received that day from Jim's father, who had attempted to write a few sentences using the smattering of Spanish he could remember. As Pete read the fractured Spanish to the group—without saying a word as to who wrote it—everybody cracked up. Without a second's hesitation Jim said, "That sounds just like Dad!"

Once Pete and I were alone, I told him how I really felt. Standing in the dark bedroom, with the sounds of others moving about the house, I said, "Pete, I'm so fearful of what might happen. Those Indians seemed friendly, but how can you be sure they won't turn on you?" I was glad for the darkness so Pete could not see my tears. I knew how important it was for him to go, and I didn't want to hold him back. But neither could I hold back my fear.

"Darling, at times my own heart begins to falter," he said softly, "but when I saw the stuffed toucan hanging in the McCullys' washroom it reminded me of God's care even for the birds. Surely he will care for us. God will not require our lives for fifty Aucas. We can trust him."

It was the first hint I'd heard that Pete also felt afraid. I took some comfort in knowing I wasn't alone, but even with his reassuring word, and our time of prayer together that night, we slept fitfully. I couldn't bring myself to ask him what I should do if he didn't come back. The sleepless night, along with the flu, made me feel worse in the morning.

Early on Tuesday morning, January 3, Johnny Keenan, the other MAF pilot, flew to Arajuno with some brake fluid Nate needed. This gave me the opportunity to fly back with him to Shell Mera to stay with Marj and see a doctor. The men were busy fixing up the plane and lugging supplies out to the airstrip.

"I don't think I will ever see you again," I said through my tears.

There on the airstrip, he hugged and kissed me good-bye. "I'll be back, darling, don't worry. I know you'd feel different if you weren't feeling sick. Dr. Johnston will fix you up and then you can come back out here [to Arajuno]. I'm glad you'll be with Marj."

The last time I saw Pete, he was standing on the grassy airstrip next to Nate's yellow Piper Cub plane. He waved to me as Johnny and I taxied down the strip for takeoff.

All the flights out to the beach with the men and supplies went according to schedule. Jim, Ed, and Roger stayed in the tree house, while Pete flew back to Arajuno with Nate each night. On Wednesday, Pete saw the Indians for the first time as he and Nate flew over the Auca village, calling over a loudspeaker for them to come to the beach. He was thrilled at last to see what Ed and Jim had seen for the past two months.

Pete wrote in his diary about the promising events that occurred on Friday: "Aucas—This is a great day for the advance of the gospel . . . An Auca voice boomed out a barrage of unintelligible excited sounds to give us the long-awaited and much-prayed-for first contact with these savages." Then three naked Aucas, two women and a man, stepped out into the open on the opposite bank. Pete's heart "jumped and thumped wildly as we walked slowly to join Ed [who had waded into the river] and to shout phrases with him." It appeared that the younger woman, dubbed "Delilah," was being offered as a gift to the missionaries.

While Pete and the other men stayed behind with the two Auca women, Nate took the Auca man, whom they had nicknamed "George," for a ride over the village in his plane. The men took lots of pictures, which Nate brought back with him to Arajuno, as he had done each night. Also upon his return, Nate had assumed the role of historian, carefully documenting each day's activities.

Meanwhile, in Shell Mera, I also felt Nate's excitement of spending the entire day Friday with three Aucas as I listened in on his radio contacts with Marj. How could we not rejoice with them? Imagine, a savage Indian man riding over his village in a plane, shouting with glee all the way. These Aucas had even eaten a white man's hamburger! They seemed to have no fear. And as I heard the reports of their astonishingly friendly interactions with the men, my own fears subsided somewhat. I even felt a little ashamed that I had been so anxious, that perhaps I had not really trusted God to do the impossible.

But rather than disappear, my fear chose to lurk beneath the surface—until the middle of the night on Friday, when a terrifying dream jolted me awake. (I knew it was significant because I rarely recall dreams.) I saw Nate's plane on the beach, and five dead bodies around it. It felt so real that I couldn't calm myself down. I had been excited for the men earlier that evening; my hope had been renewed. Why the dream?

On the beach, the men waited for the Indians to return on Saturday, but no one came. When Nate and Pete flew over their village to check on them, Nate reported to Marj some signs of fear: the women and children ran to hide. On a second and a third flight, "George," their Auca visitor from the day before, appeared, and his fairly warm response encouraged them. Perhaps the Indians would visit on Sunday and invite them to their village.

Sunday morning, as Nate and Pete climbed into the plane, Pete called to Barbara and Marilou in Arajuno: "So long, girls. Pray. I believe today's the day."

First the men flew to Palm Beach and talked over their plans for the day. Then Nate took a quick survey flight alone over the village. He saw only a few women and children at the houses, but on the way back he spotted a group of Auca men making their way toward the river. At 12:30, Nate jubilantly announced over the radio to Marj that there would be a "Sunday afternoon service," and that he would contact her again at 4:30 P.M.

For the afternoon, we chatted with the house guests and wondered how the men were doing. At 4:30, I went to the radio room with Marj, eager to hear what had happened that afternoon. She switched it on, picked up the mike as usual, and listened.

The radio remained strangely silent.

Two or three long minutes passed. Marj, looking upset, checked her watch again and said, "Nate is always right on time."

Standing there next to her, I didn't worry immediately. I tried to imagine the men's thrill on the beach at meeting all those Indians. "Marj, I'll bet the Indians came and with all the excitement the fellows forgot the radio, or maybe they actually went to their village."

"No, Nate would never do that," Marj answered emphatically. "He always keeps radio contact with me. It's like a law. You don't forget."

After a few minutes, Barbara and Marilou radioed from Arajuno, wondering if we'd heard anything yet.

As Marj kept repeating, "Shell Mera standing by—come in, Palm Beach," my heart began to sink. We prayed for Nate's voice to come over the speaker.

Silence.

"Do you think there's something wrong with their radio?" I asked, grasping at straws.

"No," Marj said again. There was a heaviness in her voice. "There are two radios on the beach, so even if one didn't work the other would."

Then she looked at me and said, "Olive, something has happened. Nate would never leave the plane there overnight. It is getting almost too late for him to fly to Arajuno and land there before dark, and still he has not radioed in." Her worried expression and serious tone scared me; I had never seen her like that. The impact of her words made me feel dazed.

As darkness fell, she turned off the radio.

"Olive, I think we should keep this to ourselves tonight," she said. "There is no point in upsetting the guests when we don't know what has happened." Easier said than done. Art Johnston, the mission doctor from HCJB in Quito who had cared for me during my second miscarriage, was working in the area and stopped by to check on me. As soon as he saw us, he knew something was wrong. We couldn't hide the truth from him. He listened carefully, then turned to me and said, "No wonder you're feeling sick."

We tried to keep busy that evening, covering up our troubled emotions the best we could. I helped Marj set the hair of one of the guests.

Whatever could have happened to them? I wondered in bed that night. Hoping for some kind of comfort from the Bible, I looked at the passage Pete and I would have read together that day for devotions. I was struck by a verse in 2 Corinthians: "He

203

who has prepared you for this very thing is God" (5:5). Musing on all the years of turmoil that I had experienced with Pete, I wondered if God had used those hard times to prepare me for this—whatever this was. All I could think of was the horrifying image of my dream. What if I really had to face what I saw in that dream tomorrow? Would I be prepared?

19
WIDOWED

*T*he next morning, Johnny Keenan flew over the Curaray River to look for the men. He located Nate's plane sitting on Palm Beach, but it had been stripped of all its fabric. He found no sign of life. Marj received his radio report at 9:30. Over the next few hours, word of the five missing missionaries was sent to the United States Air Rescue Service in the Canal Zone. Radio station HCJB in Quito broadcast the news around the world. A small group of Quichua Indians quietly left Arajuno by canoe to search the Curaray River for the men.

If I had not written down some of my thoughts that week, the blur of events and the numbness of grief would have erased all my specific memories. The verse in 2 Corinthians I had read Sunday night—even though taken out of context—brought some comfort. During those days of uncertainty I wrote of God's comfort and grace. I was confident of the Lord's leading in Pete's life to go on Operation Auca. At the same time I wrote of my own inadequacies and elevated Pete to a place of perfection in comparison. I was sure I was being punished for my own lack of faith. At times I had no hope and at other times I prayed that God would give him back to me.

When Barbara and Marilou were flown in from Arajuno on Monday, I took one look at their faces and knew they didn't realize how serious the situation was. They still hoped the men had escaped. In fact, Marilou quickly returned to Arajuno in case the men would return there on foot. By then many people were praying for the men's safety. That evening some of our missionary colleagues, including Dee Short and Dr. Johnston, and thirteen volunteer Ecuadorian soldiers began to form a ground rescue party.

On Tuesday Betty arrived from Shandia, along with Rachel Saint, Nate's sister. It was the first time I had met Rachel, and I felt very sorry for her since she had known nothing of Operation Auca until yesterday. (The men had told no one about their plans, not even their families in the States. They had believed that secrecy was of utmost importance.) That night our hopes were raised when someone reported seeing a fire in the jungles. I prayed that God would allow at least some of the men to survive. Surely God would not encourage us falsely. Surely he was in control. But the specter of my dream also haunted me; I had difficulty believing that the men were still alive. So I wavered between hope and despair.

At one point, I pled with God to bring Pete back for the Quichua work. Then, realizing that I really wanted him back for *me,* I felt guilty, as if it were somehow selfish to miss my husband. My thoughts leaped from one extreme to another as I tried to understand why this had happened. I couldn't believe God would allow the sacrifice of five men for only fifty Indians.

Despair settled in the next day, however, when Johnny found the first body floating facedown in the Curaray. Khaki pants indicated it probably wasn't Roger; Barbara said she knew Roj had worn blue jeans. But we had no other information; we could only wait, anxious and heavy-hearted.

On Thursday the Air Force Rescue personnel, led by Major Nurnberg and Navy Captain DeWitt, joined the search by helicopter. When they returned to Shell Mera later in the afternoon, someone told Johnny to bring Marilou from Arajuno. I will never forget her face as she came up the steps of the Saints' house. This time all hope had vanished.

"Do you know they are all gone?" she said through her tears.

We braced ourselves for the announcement as Major Nurnberg and Captain DeWitt asked us to gather in Marj's bedroom. They told us that four bodies had been spotted from the air. Meanwhile, the missionary ground party, which had set out early that morning, met the group of Quichua Indians returning from Palm Beach. The Indians had found Ed's body the day before in shallow water. They had brought back his watch for identification, and Major Nurnberg had picked it up by helicopter. But today the current had swept Ed's body away. That meant all five men were dead.

"All four bodies were in the water," I wrote afterward. "One, only the feet showed above the water. All were wearing tee shirts, two with light tan pants and one with blue jeans. Roj had blue jeans. One had a reddish belt. That was Pete without a doubt." Positive identification came on Friday, after the helicopter returned from the beach with the rings, watches, and notebooks from the bodies.

In my numbness I experienced an incredible feeling of rest. "Just to know is a relief," I wrote. The days had been long, the wait and strain almost unbearable. It had been easy to imagine the worst. "I am comforted to know Pete died doing the will of his Father," I continued to write. "He died just the way he wanted to."

That night I wrote down a song Pete used to sing:

Lord, in the fullness of my might,
I would for Thee be strong;

While runneth o'er each dear delight,
To Thee should soar my song.

I would not give the world my heart,
And then profess Thy love;
I would not feel my strength depart,
And then Thy service prove.

I would not with swift winged zeal
On the world's errands go;
And labour up the heav'nly hill
With weary feet and slow

O not for Thee my weak desires,
My poorer baser part!
O not for Thee my fading fires,
The ashes of my heart.

O choose me in my golden time.
In my dear joys have part!
For Thee the glory of my prime,
The fullness of my heart.

When the military men and the missionary ground party returned from Palm Beach, we listened as they described the terrible rain storm that had struck just as they were burying the bodies. The sky was so dark and the rain so heavy that they could hardly see. Fear dominated their thoughts; they said they could sense the presence of evil. They always kept their guns pointed toward the jungles.

The rescue service personnel marveled at the reaction of the five women and nine children. They had expected to find five hysterical wives, a common scene in their various rescue missions. But God kept us calm, at least on the outside. There was too much to do—children to care for, people to feed, briefings with the search parties, decisions to make. And all the while, *Life* magazine photographer Cornell Capa ran around taking hundreds of pictures, including the famous photo of Dr. Johnston talking to us in the Saints' kitchen. (Elisabeth Elliot's *Through Gates of Splendor* describes most of these day-to-day details.) Before the military people left, they flew us over Palm Beach in a Navy plane to see the common grave where the men had been hastily buried.

The following week, local missionaries conducted a simple memorial service at a small mission Bible school. Representatives from all three missions of the five men—the Gospel Missionary Union, Missionary Aviation Fellowship, and Christian Missions in Many Lands (the Brethren missions organization), flew in from the States. Relatives and friends arrived to give us much-needed counsel and assistance with decisions we had never faced before. Each visitor filled some special need for us at that time. We were always conscious of people praying for us, and noticed that God had given us the strength and peace we needed. For the past week we had hoped that the fellows would be found alive. When they weren't, we gave up that temporal hope and we grieved, but thankfully we never lost our eternal hope in Christ.

Many nationals who came to comfort us found it hard to understand why we did not have the bodies brought out from the jungles. They didn't realize how difficult this task would have been. Only a tiny helicopter could land on the beach now, precluding an evacuation by air. And carrying four bodies for several days on the river and over muddy trails was unthinkable. Besides, the bodies were already decomposing after sitting in water for almost a week in a tropical climate. We explained to the nationals that the body did not matter as much to us as the assurance from God's Word that the men's souls were in heaven. But some of them still felt we did not care about our husbands because we had left their bodies in the jungles.

For a Christian, death is not the end. Rather it is a door,

the grand entryway into heaven. But it is heaven, not death, that we look forward to. Not until we encounter death, however, does heaven become a real place to us. Amid all the grief and all the activity, the five of us talked about heaven and wondered aloud what the men would be doing. Would they know what was happening here on earth? (We wanted them to know we were doing all right.) Would they know they were with the Lord? Would they be talking to him? We asked all kinds of questions. So little is known about heaven except for our images of gold streets and many mansions. But we knew the Lord was there. "Wouldn't it be wonderful if the Lord came back to take us right now?" one of the women said.

Unfortunately, that did not happen. Life would move on, and we would have to move with it. Marilou had to decide right away where to have her baby. She chose to return to the States. We all went with her to Arajuno to help her pack up their personal belongings. She gave away most of the equipment to other missionaries working in the jungles. Soon the house Ed had built stood empty of all but the past year's memories. No doubt she recalled the Indians standing around, always watching; Stevie riding his tricycle from room to room; Ed's excitement upon returning from his bucket-drop flights with Nate; the last "pow wow" when we all talked about Operation Auca; and Christmas barely three weeks before with the Flemings and the Elliots and the little Christmas tree she had set up. But now it was over, never to be repeated. Marilou was the first of the widows to leave. When she and the two children boarded the plane after a tearful good-bye, she didn't know whether she'd ever return.

Though I sensed God's presence and support much of the time, I also struggled with many dark feelings. I couldn't understand why Pete and I had gone through a difficult breakup, a long time apart with no assurance of the future, two miscarriages once we finally got together—and now he was gone. At times I was overwhelmed by loneliness. I realized how dependent I was on Pete, and the longer I was without him, the more inadequate I felt.

I tried to be "strong" because it was somehow expected of me; showing emotion apparently diluted one's Christian witness before others. But at times grief washed over me in waves, and I could not hold back the tears. On one such occasion, Betty, who had remained stoic through the whole ordeal, chided me: "You are just feeling sorry for yourself," she said. "It isn't out of love for Pete that you're crying." I could only think of Jesus weeping at his friend Lazarus's death. I had to cry; the tears were a necessary emotional release for me. Yet even in these dark moments, God brought me comfort as I read the Scriptures.

To our surprise, we began to hear that newspapers across the United States had carried reports of the five missionaries' death. "How little did we realize," I wrote in my journal, "that such a small operation of five men in a little plane reaching a small Indian group would have been heard of by so many people." As I thought of reaching a world beyond that of the Aucas, I found it easier to accept that God was somehow involved in it all. I prayed that everyone who heard the story would be touched.

As for the Aucas themselves, after killing the men, they had disappeared once again into the jungles. It seemed hopeless now that we would ever reach them. We wondered if they had seen the helicopter and the huge Navy plane, and if so, what they must have thought. Had they been watching the rescue parties from hidden jungle posts, and witnessed the soldiers and their guns? We also wondered if all the men's work had been wasted.

A few weeks later, Rachel Saint, who had been working with Dayuma, the Auca girl from Ila, showed Dayuma the pictures the men had taken on the beach. Amazingly, Dayuma recognized the older Auca woman as her mother's sister, and was excited to know that at least one of her relatives was alive. It gave her hope that perhaps her mother might be, too. I wondered if one day Dayuma (who was not yet a Christian) might be a link to bring the gospel to the Aucas.

Everywhere I went, I faced the anguish of Pete's death all over again. When I arrived back in Shandia with Betty, the Indians, who had not seen us since the men were killed, expressed their sorrow the only way they knew—by wailing. I remembered Pete's journal entry about the eeriness and hopelessness of their wailing. One of the older Indian women sat next to me and said, "Poor Senora, your Pedro is gone and you do not even have a child."

Widowhood is probably the last thing a young woman wants to talk about —unless she is a widow herself. One day in Shandia, Betty and I talked about missing the fellows and about our own new status.

"It's so hard to believe that we're no longer wives but widows," I said. "The only widows I have known have been old."

"Do you think you will remarry?" Betty answered. "I think you will, as well as some of the others."

"I can't even imagine remarrying," I said. "Can you?" I already knew what her answer would be.

"No, Jim was the only one for me. Have you read what Paul wrote in First Corinthians 7 to the unmarried and widows? 'It is well for them to remain single, as I do. But if they cannot exercise self-control, they should marry. For it is better to marry than to to be aflame with passion.' What do you think that means?"

"I never gave it much thought," I replied. "I guess you don't until you're one of them."

We then carried on a brief theological discussion about whether young widows should remarry. We never did settle the question.

While in Shandia with Betty, I noticed a gradual change in my outlook. As I read various selections from Amy Carmichael's book, *His Thoughts Said . . . His Father Said,* I came across one entitled, "In Acceptance Lieth Peace." I knew long before going to Ecuador that if the Aucas were found, Pete would go to reach them. He had committed himself to that end in what he believed was obedience to God's call. It occurred to me that God had somehow prepared each one of the men for this mission. Standing at the edge of the cliff, gazing down at the Napo River, I remembered the flood that had destroyed virtually all the work Jim and Pete had invested in Shandia. Yet through all their experiences, they had trusted God. Now I was questioning why God would cut short the work he had prepared me for. Was it time for me to trust God too, just as Jim and Pete had? Though I hadn't yet decided what to do with my life, that day I once again committed my uncertain future to God.

Back in December, while the plans for Operation Auca were still coming together, I had told Betty that I would probably go home if Pete were killed. Now I actually had to face that decision. I knew I would have serious difficulty learning the Quichua language, which still had not been completely reduced to writing. And I wasn't sure I could live in the high altitude of Quito after experiencing so much sickness there. I simply didn't know whether I had a future in Ecuador. I decided to leave the question open and return to the States for a while, especially since money had been sent to me for that purpose.

First I had to close the station at Puyupungu and pack up my belongings. Betty came along to help and to tell the Indians all that had happened. Again we had to relive all the wrenching emotions. We couldn't have escaped or forgotten them even if we had wanted to. But verses of Scripture came to mind, assuring me of God's presence. With the help of a new type of plane from Wycliffe, and pilot Larry Montgomery, we moved my few belongings from Puyupungu to Shell Mera. Then I flew to Quito.

On February 16 in Quito, the president of Ecuador recognized the sacrifice of the five missionaries in a special ceremony. Marj Saint, Barbara Youderian, and I, along with the directors of several mission organizations, attended a reception at the president's palace. He praised the efforts of the five men and presented a plaque in honor of all the evangelical missions in Ecuador. The door to missions in that small country had opened wider.

The subject of widowhood came up again just before I left Quito for the States. While visiting the landlady of the apartment Pete and I had lived in just before going to the jungles, she and her mother (a widow herself) told me, "You are too young to be a widow. Don't stay here. It is very hard and sad to be a widow here. Once a widow, always a widow. Go back to the United States and marry again." Apparently, people thought they were comforting me by assuring me that I was young and would remarry. But at the time, I found this "comfort" hard to handle.

On the plane home, I had my first experience with the negative effects of publicity. The flight attendant, seeing from my ring that I was married but that my husband was not with me, made snide remarks about my traveling alone. When I told him what had happened, he bluntly replied that the men deserved to be killed. He had no use for missionaries. Then he learned from another passenger that the story had appeared in *Life*. "That is one way to get money for your mission!" he muttered. For the rest of the flight I had to endure all his grievances with religion, church, and missions. No matter what I said, he concluded that it all boiled down to a desire for money. By the time we landed, I had convinced him that the men were sincere, but I began to wonder if God would be able to use the men's story in people's lives. The flight attendant's skepticism prepared me for other skeptics I would face in the years to come.

In Seattle, my parents bathed me in love and support, and suggested I live with them for the time being. They told me they had already received crank calls from con artists attempting to take advantage of people in mourning.

I also visited Pete's folks right away, because I had heard about the awful way they had learned of Pete's death. They had not even known that the Aucas had been found. It was two days after the five men disappeared that a telegram arrived at their home saying that the five men were missing. But it had been mistakenly addressed to the Elliots, which only confused the Flemings further. Then, they had hardly finished reading the telegram when reporters showed up at the front door. When I finally arrived and went to see them, they were in deep sorrow. I explained that Pete had been unable to write about the mission because of their concern for secrecy. I also made it clear that Pete had decided on his own to go, and that Jim had tried to dissuade him. By telling them the full story, I managed to bring them a little comfort.

For the next nine months, my calendar was filled with speaking engagements, mostly to Christian women's groups, youth groups, and conferences. I addressed many kinds of people—some who, like the flight attendant, were skeptical of what the five men did, and others who saw their death as a great triumph for the cause of Christ. Encouraging letters came in from people around the world who had been deeply moved by the account of the five men. I discovered that newspapers and magazines around the globe had carried the story.

Nearly a year had passed since Pete and the men were killed. But I still hadn't settled on what to do with my life. In December 1956, I returned to Ecuador with Marilou McCully, who had decided to establish a home for missionary children to stay in while they attended school in Quito. I went to help her with her two young boys and baby on the long flight to Ecuador, as well as during the setup of the home. But I also took time to consider my own future as a missionary there. After much prayer and counsel, I decided to return to the States. With great difficulty I managed to go through our wedding gifts (they had been stored in Shell Mera) and give them away to missionary friends. I spent that Christmas with Marilou, Marj, and Barbara in Quito. Betty had gone back to the States to meet with the publisher of her forthcoming book, *Through Gates of Splendor,* but she returned to Ecuador after Christmas and we all met together. (Not since then have all five widows been reunited.)

Just before I left, one of the MAF pilots flew me over Auca territory one last time. As I gazed at the vast expanse of green jungles, I wondered if anyone would ever find those Indians. Had all the efforts of the men gone to waste? We prepared to turn back when, just ahead of us, we spotted a small clearing next to a river. We circled around for a closer look. It was an Auca house.

20
THE RETURN

*I*n the months and years following Pete's death, so many questions had filled my mind: Why did this have to happen? Was God responsible, or did the men commit a fatal error? Should they have waited for a better time? Exactly what happened when the men met the Aucas? Should a woman have gone in first? Why did God keep Pete and me apart for so long, only to let him die shortly after we married? Should Pete even have gone to Ecuador at all, when his health and his gifts seemed to point elsewhere? Was the death of five men really necessary in order to reach this tribe? Some of my questions were answered as new information came to light. Others, I stopped asking because I knew they could never be answered. But many of my questions remained. And in order to find the answers—or at least to make peace with my questions—I knew that one day I would go back to Ecuador.

On January 8, 1989, thirty-three years to the day after the men were killed, my dream came true.

In that span of time my life had moved in a new direction. I was now the wife of Dr. Walter Liefeld, professor of New Testament at Trinity Evangelical Divinity School, and lived in the comfortable Chicago suburb of Deerfield. Walt and I had brought up three children in our thirty years of marriage. Our oldest, David, an engineer, was contemplating marriage to Robin Lettman. Our daughter, Beverly, a nurse, had been married for two years to Jonathan Hancock, a pastor at LaSalle Street Church in Chicago. Our youngest was twenty-year-old Holly, a sophomore at Illinois State University. I had enjoyed a rich and fulfilling life with my family, and had continued speaking to student and church groups.

Life for the Auca Indians had changed, too. The Auca house I had seen on that last flight in early 1957 marked the beginning of a new attempt to reach that tribe. MAF pilot Johnny Keenan had picked up where Nate Saint left off and had continued to make the bucket-style gift drops. One day two Auca women had appeared at a Quichua village near Arajuno. When Betty, who just "happened" to be visiting Arajuno at the time, got word of this development, she had immediately left for the village. To her amazement, one of the women was Dayuma's aunt—the older woman who had met the five men on the beach. These two women had served as the bridge for Betty and later Dayuma and Rachel to make contact with the Aucas. Eventually, many of the scattered Auca groups had become Christians, including all five of the actual killers. Three of them had even become pastors to their own tribe. The ancient traditions of terror and murder had been broken. The Aucas were now called by their real name, the Waorani (wah-oh-RAH-nee), rather than the Quichua name of Auca, which means "savage."

On the flight down to Ecuador, I reflected on all these changes. Now, at last, I was returning to visit the people of my past. How would I feel toward them? Would it just be opening old wounds?

Walt, Holly, and I arrived in Quito on Sunday—not only the same date, but the same day of the week that Pete had been killed. One of the first people to greet us was Rachel Saint, who has remained with the Waorani Indians for more than thirty years. She would accompany us to the jungles to visit the Waoranis. Driving through Quito, I marveled at how it had grown into a modern, bustling city. That first evening, Walt and I spoke to the English Fellowship Church. I described my dark feelings on this very night when Pete had been missing, and told how God had remained faithful after thirty-three years. As I looked out over the congregation, several familiar faces from long ago reminded me of all who had helped us during those difficult days of waiting.

If time had changed Quito for the better, I realized it had virtually stood still outside of the city. Much of the narrow mountain road to Shell Mera, where the Andes mountains meet the jungles, was still unpaved and only wide enough for one truck. Among all the bumps and other obstacles, our van splashed through small streams that crossed the road, and passed under a gentle waterfall which no doubt became a mighty force in a torrential downpour. The well-seasoned missionary takes these muddy, bone-jarring roads in stride, but first-time travelers may wonder whether one trip is enough. With all the rain and erosion, I could hardly believe the road still existed. (We later learned that the annual rainfall in Shell Mera is twenty-one *feet,* a fact that had eluded me years before.)

This treacherous road no longer ends at Shell Mera, but continues on to some of the jungle towns and stations which years ago could only be accessed by plane. But one must still fly, or walk for many days over the trail, to reach the Waorani. Knowing that the rainy season would begin soon, I had feared that conditions would prevent us from flying into the jungles. At Shell Mera we boarded a larger, sleeker MAF plane (much nicer than the tiny Piper Cub Nate flew) along with Rachel and the pilot, and took off. Our destination was the Waorani village of Toñampare, where Rachel lived and worked.

Because of our tight schedule and an approaching storm, we had to settle for a bird's eye view of Puyupungu and Arajuno. From the air they looked much the same as when I left. Then we headed over Waorani territory in a course not unlike Nate Saint's. On my last flight over this forbidden realm, I had felt overwhelmed by sadness and failure. Now, as I gazed at the lush, unbroken rain forests below, I was filled with great anticipation. Soon I would see for myself how the lives of these once elusive and dangerous people had changed.

Circling over the Curaray River, we caught a glimpse of Palm Beach before landing at Toñampare. Immediately I recalled my flight in the Navy plane when I first saw that beach. With only a ring, a watch, and a belt as identification, I had found it hard to grasp that Pete was really dead. But actually seeing the beach with the destroyed plane and the common grave had brought the reality home. Then, the beach had been a place of death. Now there was no sign that anyone had ever walked upon it. All the sandbars looked alike.

As we landed in the village of Toñampare, the Indians gathered at the airstrip and the children came running toward the plane. How typical! The coming of the MAF plane had always been a big event at the jungle stations. My heart raced as I scanned the crowd, wondering whether I'd recognize Dayuma or Kimo.

"It's like walking into the *National Geographic*," Holly said, interrupting my musing. I had been so lost in memories that it hadn't occurred to me what my family might be thinking.

With the warm welcome we received, I knew Rachel had prepared them for our coming. I had to remind myself that these people had once been the feared Aucas. A few Quichua Indians also lived here, I was told, but they could not be distinguished from the younger Waoranis, since the former Auca trademark, a large hole in each earlobe holding a plug of balsa wood, was no longer used. The older Waorani could not hide those large holes, which now hung empty and limp. Unlike thirty years ago, everyone wore simple, western clothes—the men, trousers and teeshirts or sport shirts, and the women, loose dresses. Just to see Quichuas and Waoranis— once deadly enemies—now living together in peace, was in itself a miracle.

As I surveyed the Indians along the airstrip, I recognized Dayuma—now in her fifties—standing with her grown son, Sam. So much had happened to both of us since I last saw her. I remembered Rachel showing her the pictures the five men had taken of the friendly Aucas on the beach, and Dayuma's excitement as she recognized the older woman as her aunt. Since that time she has played a key role in reaching her people with the gospel (see *The Dayuma Story,* by Ethel Emily Wallis). Even today, Dayuma is a leader among the Waoranis.

Next we were greeted by Kimo, a member of the attack party in 1956. Rachel had thoughtfully arranged for him and his wife Dawa to be flown here from their distant village. They had agreed to take us to Palm Beach. Walt and I recalled the first time we had met Kimo back in 1967. Rachel had brought Kimo and Dayuma's husband, Komi, to the World Congress on Evangelism in Berlin. Afterward they had traveled to the United States, and we had met them in Chicago. (Komi, though not one of the killers, was the son of Gikita, the oldest man in the tribe and the leader of the band that had killed not only the missionaries, but other Aucas as well.)

Over the next few days, the changing history of the Waoranis that I had only read about became tangible. We saw several Indians who had suffered from the 1969 polio epidemic. At that time, many had died and others were paralyzed. We had prayed for the survival of the tribe and for Rachel's protection from the white man's disease. Now, as we encountered an Indian in a wheelchair (a strange sight in the jungles, I might add), we realized that his very presence testified to the change God had brought to this tribe. Why? Previously, a man who could not traverse the muddy jungle trails to work and hunt might have been killed off as a burden. But no longer.

Many Indians gathered at Rachel's house to see her foreign visitors. Rachel had told them who I was, but quickly introduced "Dr. Walter" as my "new" husband (of thirty-one years!) and a Bible teacher. The Indians watched Holly trying with some difficulty to lie across a hammock Indian-style. Once she had settled in, Kimo announced, "She has come well. She sits in the hammock, swinging happily." The babies and young children, frightened by our appearance—and especially by Holly's long blond hair—clung to their mothers and cried. Since the Indians are quite short, our height probably scared them as well. But within a short time, the children had relaxed and learned Holly's name. After dark, they would come up to the door and call her name, only to run away in glee when she answered.

Sometimes the three of us sat around with the Indians and tried to communicate. After watching one of the women weave a basket, Holly tried it herself.

"This is *hard*," she said. "How do they do it?" The Indians laughed as they looked on. They couldn't understand how white people could be so inept. Weaving a basket was so simple to them.

"I'm learning more in these three days," Holly remarked, "than in a whole semester of cross-cultural communications class in college."

One highlight of our visit to Toñampare was attending church with the Waoranis. They asked Walt and me to speak to the group.

"I prayed many years for the day when I could come to see you," I began, pausing for Rachel's translation. "I first heard about you many years ago and started to pray for you. Even though I prayed for you I was fearful of your people. When the men flew over your houses and saw your people, and saw how you even built platforms and sent back gifts, they thought you wanted to be friends. But you were afraid of us."

As soon as I mentioned the platforms, a discussion erupted among the men over just who built the platforms and why.

Then I continued: "God has answered our prayers for you. Our fear of each other is gone. I thank God for you. Even though my first husband never was able to tell you about God, my second husband is here to talk to you from God's Word."

Rachel again introduced "Dr. Walter," the Bible teacher. Walt told the Indians two stories from the Bible, each one about a son who had died. From the Old Testament, he told of Elisha and the widow's son. God had given a child to the woman who was kind to Elisha. But when the child died, Elisha had brought it back to life through the power of God. From the New Testament, Walt gave the account of the widow of Nain's son: "Several hundred years later, the Jewish people built another village on a different part of the same mountain. One day Jesus came to that village and saw a woman who was a widow. She was coming out of the village to bury her son who had died. Jesus brought that son back to life."

The Waorani congregation listened intently. Walt went on to talk about the power of Jesus, God's Son. He related how Jesus, who was a completely good man, "let himself be captured by his enemies and let them kill him on the cross" for our sins. "And when we tell God that we are sorry for our sins, and thank Jesus for dying in our place, God forgives all our sins." Discreetly referring to Pete's death, he said that one day we must all face death; but through Christ we can be alive forever in God's beautiful heaven. As he referred to John 3:16, immediately the whole group of Waoranis recited the verse aloud.

When Walt finished, Kimo prayed a long prayer. The only words we recognized were "Waorani" and "Amen." For all his years of teaching and preaching, Walt had never spoken to such a primitive group. Rachel told us afterward that his words would be indelibly marked on their minds, and would be carried to other Waorani groups throughout the forest.

As Rachel said this, I was suddenly overcome by emotion, struck by the thrill of this moment in contrast to the pain and disappointment of the past. Pete had prayed for so long to have the privilege of teaching these people, yet had never received the opportunity. Now Walt had been given that privilege. Would I ever understand God's ways?

Meanwhile, there was great excitement outside the church. Another group had just arrived on foot: an Indian man, several young Indian women, and an older woman. They lived a two-day walk away, but by starting at night, they had made it here in a day and a half—even more of an undertaking since one woman carried a baby. (Rachel had radioed them of our visit, but hadn't heard whether they would be able to come.) After watching a lively conversation between the visitors and hosts, we realized how significant these people were in the ongoing story that began with the five slain missionaries. The women came from another Waorani group of Christians, and the man, Tamanta, was their pastor. To our joyful surprise, we learned that Tamanta was the son of "George" of Palm Beach. The oldest woman, Oncaye, originally belonged to the down-river Auca group, a group once so savage that they were feared even by other Aucas. Seeing these faithful Christians was more than we had hoped for.

They had come especially to see us, and we felt honored. With Rachel's help, I greeted them as I did the others in church. I repeated that we no longer had fear of each other but now we were in God's family, brothers and sisters in the Lord.

Then Tamanta spoke. After reading Mark 6:30 from the

Waorani text about the crowds that gathered around Jesus, he said, "When you were coming out of the church and we were just arriving, you were all talking at once. It was just like that when Jesus saw all the people. They were coming and going so he took his disciples off where they could sit down and listen and have some rest." His words seemed fitting after we heard about their long, arduous trip. ("We came fast and all this crowd are aching," he explained.) As I listened to Tamanta, I thought of his father, the first Auca man to meet the five missionaries, and the only one to meet them without a spear. "George" died before he knew why they had come.

Tamanta had played a key role in helping Catherine Peeke of Wycliffe to translate the Bible into Waorani. Catherine, who along with Rachel was one of the first Wycliffe translators in Ecuador, has lived in these jungles since the early 1950s. Once Betty left the work in Ecuador, Catherine worked with Rachel on reducing the language to writing and translating the Scriptures—a long and laborious process that continues to this day. "Soon we will have all the books of the New Testament in Waorani," Tamanta happily announced.

That night a group of us sat in Rachel's house, some around the table, others on the hammocks or stools, and listened to Oncaye's and Dawa's animated accounts of life in a savage Auca tribe. Though Walt and I couldn't understand a word they said, we were mesmerized by the drama of their expressions, their laughter, their imitations—twigs breaking, animal sounds, and rain falling—and their constant gesturing, which cast shadows across the candle-lit room. Amid all the sounds and motions, Rachel tried to keep us up with the narratives.

I was astonished at the number of killings within the families and groups of Waorani themselves. Oncaye said she had felt more afraid of her own family than of cannibals in the outside world. After watching her own brother spear her grandmother to death, she was so filled with grief and fear that she began to look for a better way to live. She decided to flee during an Auca raid, but was instead shot and left to die. "Foreigners" picked her up, however, and nursed her back to health. Eventually she came to live with Rachel, and became a Christian. As she spoke, I suddenly realized she was the young Auca girl found wounded at the Napo River, for whom I had prayed many years ago.

Once Oncaye found Christ, she had set out to find the rest of her family, still living as savages, so she could share the gospel of peace with them. Dawa, a relative of Oncaye, accompanied Oncaye on many daring attempts to find her people. (Before the original band of Aucas who killed the five missionaries had been reached with the gospel, they had murdered Dawa's parents and forced her to return to their village, where she later married Kimo. Dawa had later been the first Auca to embrace Christ, followed by Kimo and the others, when Dayuma first introduced Him to the Aucas.)

Together they recounted story after story to us, usually speaking simultaneously, which made it difficult for Rachel to keep up with the translating. Many of the accounts sounded familiar, as I remembered reading them in the book *Aucas Downriver,* by Ethel Emily Wallis. On one of their treks over unfamiliar terrain—alone and unarmed—they discovered that a jaguar was following them. Realizing that they might be forced to fight it off, they found comfort in the Bible story in which God helped David kill a lion. I shuddered to hear such a practical application of Scripture.

At the very moment Oncaye (accompanied by Dawa, Kimo, and Dyuwi, another of the killers who had converted to Christ) finally found her family, her brother's wife was dying from a snake bite. But providentially, they had brought snake bite serum with them—at Rachel's insistence. Without this serum, Oncaye's sister-in-law would have died. Even more remarkable, the frightened Indians allowed Dawa to give the serum injections, which they had never heard of, and then permitted Kimo, their archenemy, to carry her fifty miles to Rachel, one of the "foreigners" they feared most of all.

What motivated these Indians to risk their lives again and again to reach the downriver people? I wondered. Family? True, Oncaye had wanted to see her mother, but she had continued her relentless efforts even after she thought her mother had been killed. Further, something more than family ties must have led Dawa, Kimo, and Dyuwi to endanger their lives as well. The motivation had to have come from within: a God-given love and a deep desire to share with their fierce relatives the new life they had in Jesus.

The strong faith and the prominent role of these two women amazed me. They were much more than storytellers: they were truly the key for reaching the various groups. Almost every successful entrance into a new group of Waoranis came through one of these women. They had to make the initial contacts in order to convince a group that they were friendly. Once that was accomplished, the men, who came along but hid nearby, could appear.

(Not until after I returned home and reread *Aucas Downriver* did I realize the accuracy of Oncaye's storytelling after so many years. She could have easily embellished the story; instead, she gave virtually the identical account she had given to the book's author, Ethel Wallis. Like many ancient cultures, the Waorani have always passed on their history and their knowledge by oral tradition—in contrast to more advanced cultures which depend on the written word. The Waorani have no history books: it is all in their heads. That is why they can retell events in great detail, not only with correct names and places, but with all the accompanying sights and sounds. My reason for stressing this point will become clear in the next chapter.)

In the years since those initial evangelistic efforts of Oncaye, Dawa, Kimo, and Dyuwi, many Waorani groups converted to Christianity. But there were also plenty of times of discouragement, fear, and even failure. It took months and even years for the light to penetrate minds bound by darkness and evil. As one hurdle was overcome, another would appear as the Indian evangelists tried to reach a new group of Waorani. The old patterns of hatred and revenge had such a hold on many groups that it was easy for some to lapse back into old ways of thinking. For example, many groups so routinely buried a child alive with a dying parent that even professing Christians hesitated to give up the practice. Some of the Indians never left their old ways of life, and rejected the gospel outright.

Even today, some Waorani remain unreached and extremely dangerous. One particularly barbaric group of about two hundred, who live farther to the east of Ecuador in an area known as the "ridge," are a constant threat both to the friendly Waorani and to the oil company personnel who occupy the jungles around their land. As recently as 1987, this group had brutally murdered and mutilated the bodies of a well-intentioned bishop and a nun, who, in spite of Rachel's strong warnings, had visited the village.

Apparently the violent Indians who remain have become more so as outsiders occupy the land that they once roamed freely. Like the Aucas of thirty years ago, their savagery stems from fear: they consider outsiders such as the oil companies and white settlers a threat to their very survival. Ironically, the way they kill within their own family group presents a far greater threat to their existence than any outside parties. So Oncaye, Dyuwi, Dawa, Kimo, and the other Christian Waorani keep waiting and praying for a breakthrough to this part of their tribe.

Besides chronicling her many evangelistic exploits, Oncaye also talked about her faith, which was simple and solid. I was touched when she described her feelings during a severe earthquake that had hit the jungles a few years ago. Her village had been spared, but all she had thought about during the quake was that Jesus was coming to take them all to heaven to live with him. When the ground had stopped shaking and Jesus had not come, she had been disappointed. Her perspective struck me: A cataclysmic event that formerly would have wrought nothing but terror had instead filled her with hope.

When Holly and Walt and I finally went to bed, I prayed that tomorrow would be the day I had hoped for all these years—the day I would stand on Palm Beach for the very first time. Because of the Indians' relaxed attitude toward schedules, I could not be sure exactly when we'd make the trip. But I was counting on tomorrow. Exhausted after all the evening's activity, I climbed under the mosquito netting and quickly fell asleep.

21
PALM BEACH

At 4:30 on the morning of January 12, 1989, we were awakened by the sound of animals running over the roof. Instead of hearing the strange, but expected, sounds of the jungle, we heard roosters crowing and turkeys gobbling. (Because the jungle no longer supplies enough food for everyone in the village, the Waorani now keep a full farm, including ducks, chickens, and cattle.) In my excitement I could no longer sleep. Would today be the day?

By early afternoon, I learned that it was. Led by Kimo and Dawa, we followed the trail to the Curaray River through groves of banana trees and yucca planted by the Indians. At the water's edge, Dawa retrieved the narrow dugout canoe and we all climbed in: Rachel, the official guide, at the bow; the three Liefelds in the middle; and Kimo and Dawa, who held their little girl, behind us. Kimo skillfully maneuvered the canoe into the current. Ahead we noticed a threatening sky.

Fortunately, this ride did not begin to compare with my first screaming canoe trip to Puyupungu so long ago. The muddy Curaray moved more slowly than other rivers I'd seen in the jungles, though the current picked up somewhat around the bends. A disturbing thought occurred to me almost immediately: the five men's bodies had been found floating in this river, on this very day thirty-three years ago. I shivered, but then remembered we were upriver from the beach, and the bodies had been carried downriver. None of the bodies had been in this part. I also realized that when I last lived here, this very canoe trip would have been terrifying, as an Auca ambush could have occurred at any moment.

The peaceful twenty-minute excursion gave me a chance to reflect on what had happened thirty-three years ago at Palm Beach. Why was it so important for me to see the beach? Not to visit the common grave, or the remains of the tree house, as they had long since washed away. From the air, the beach had looked no different than any other beach along the Curaray. But for me Palm Beach symbolized the events that had so suddenly ended the first part of my life. It represented death, and grief, and loss.

I wondered what Kimo was thinking as he took us to the place where he had killed the missionaries. Was this difficult for him? Did he still feel guilty for what he had done? Did he fully understand the Lord's forgiveness? Had this killing been just like all the others, or had anything been different about it? As we glided in silence down the river, images of that fateful day in 1956 kept coursing through my mind.

Rachel's voice interrupted my thoughts. "The beach is just around the bend," she said, "but the rain's going to come any minute." We could even hear it pounding on the river and forest ahead of us. Quickly she pulled out the umbrellas and rain ponchos and said, "Put these on—fast." I looked up, and saw the gray sheet of rain moving our way. Walt and I worried more about the camera than ourselves.

There is no way to escape a tropical downpour. Seconds later the rain beat upon us. No matter how closely we huddled under the umbrella, or how tightly we pulled the ponchos around us, we were drenched. It struck me that the rescue team had been suddenly enveloped in just such a storm while trying to bury the bodies of the five men. The storm's violence and darkness had cast a supernatural pallor, an evil presence, over the beach. The grim reality of death and the danger of attack had only heightened these feelings.

Not so this day. Ten minutes later, when we landed at Palm Beach, the storm had nearly passed. Everything seemed very ordinary and we had no fear of attack. My first impression was, "What a mess!" Strewn with rocks and debris, the beach looked quite different from the old pictures I had of smooth sand, clear water, and tall trees. Over the years, floods had altered the river's path, cutting away much of the beach. No one had landed a plane here since 1956. High waters had ripped out the tall trees that used to line the beach, including the tree that had once held the tree house. Kimo could only point toward where it had stood. He showed us where the men had built their campfire and their small sun shelter.

Kimo also indicated where the path the Aucas had taken emerged from the forest, and commented to Rachel that if the men had set up camp even a half-mile up or down river from this trail, the Aucas would probably never have found them, as they tended to follow established trails.

So now I have seen it, I thought. I didn't feel any different. Had I expected something more—the discovery of a telltale artifact, a profound new insight, previously unknown information? I wondered if it was appropriate to ask about the moment of the killings.

Dawa must have read my mind. Without a word from us, she began to recount the events that led up to the killing. She spoke to Rachel earnestly and at great length, pausing only occasionally. I wanted to interrupt so Rachel could translate for us, but Dawa's intensity made me wait.

Eventually Rachel turned to us and said, "She is talking

about the Indians returning from the beach after they met with the foreigners. Dawa kept telling her people that the foreigners wanted to be friends, but no one listened to her. She didn't want any more killings."

After another long exchange, Rachel said, "It was when she saw the Indians kill the five foreigners on the beach that she knew for sure they really had wanted to be friends of the Waoranis."

"Did she actually see them killed?" I asked.

"Yes. I didn't know she had been here at the beach. When Gikita, the most experienced killer, and the four younger Waoranis went to the beach for the attack, Dawa and some other Indians followed and watched from the higher ground of the riverbank. The forest hid them from view, so the foreigners didn't know they were there. As she watched the Waoranis attack the foreigners with the lances, she saw that the foreigners had guns. [The Waorani knew about guns because they had seen white men use them before.] But they did not try to defend themselves; they fired the guns over the Indians' heads to frighten them. But the Waorani kept on coming anyway. Instead of shooting their attackers, the foreigners deliberately let the Waorani kill them. Dawa is saying that she knew those men could have killed the Waorani with their guns, but they didn't."

Dawa continued her story. At one point she slapped her knee and laughed, then brushed her hand against her forehead. We waited impatiently to hear what these motions meant. Rachel explained, "Dawa said that the bullets that went over the heads of the Indians on the beach went into the forest where she was hidden with the other Waoranis. One of the Waorani men was grazed on his forehead and Dawa was hit on her knee. I never heard this about Dawa."

Her account answered several unresolved questions. Soon after Betty and Rachel had begun to live with the tribe, they had heard about an Indian who had been struck in the forehead by a bullet. But they also knew the men had vowed not to use their guns against the Indians. We now understood that the man had been hit by accident. The story also explained, most likely, why the rescue party had found a bullet hole in the window of the plane.

Rachel then told us about one of her first talks with Gikita thirty years ago, before his conversion. She had explained to him that two of the five missionaries had been soldiers and could have easily killed him with their guns, but they had chosen not to. This point had deeply impressed Gikita. Rachel felt that the men's commitment to nonviolence had not only demonstrated their friendliness, but also broke the cycle of revenge. The Aucas had expected the men to retaliate, but they did not. The mindset of the Indians at that time sheds light on the men's decision to bring guns in the first place. The Aucas probably would not have noticed if the men had no guns. What ultimately impressed them, and later led to the conversion of Gikita and the other killers, was that the men had guns but refused to defend themselves.

Now both Dawa and Kimo went back to their story, speaking at the same time in good Waorani tradition. Again we marveled at all their emphatic gestures and sound effects. Rachel struggled to break into their dialogue long enough to translate without missing anything herself. She finally paused and said to us, "Dawa is telling me something I have never heard before. I have to listen closely to the two of them."

Dawa put her hand on her hip and slid it upwards several times on the outside of her skirt. Then she held out her hand, palm up. Walt and I watched Rachel's face and we tried to figure out Dawa's motion. Whatever was she saying?

Rachel listened for a while, and then related an incident that had occurred two days before the men were killed: "Dawa said that on the day the five men were visited by the three

Waorani, one of the men took something out of his body. [The Aucas, who at that time wore no clothes, apparently did not know about pockets; they thought it had come out of his body.] He held it in his hand for their Indian visitors to see." It was a photo of Dayuma. Probably the men were trying to explain that she was alive, but the photo created the opposite effect. Though the Aucas recognized Dayuma's face, they had no concept of photography; they were startled and probably frightened to see the visitor produce a little Dayuma "out of his body."

To make matters worse, the missionaries had no idea that the older woman was Dayuma's aunt, and the younger woman, "Delilah," was Dayuma's little sister, which likely added to their fear. (This was the first time I had known "Delilah's" relationship to Dayuma.) The Indians drew the only possible conclusion they could: The men had eaten Dayuma. So the three Aucas went back to the tribe that night and told everyone that the foreigners were cannibals.

According to Kimo and Dawa, the photo of Dayuma was the thing that caused the Indians to distrust and finally to kill the missionaries. We realized that the men had probably made an understandable, but fatal, mistake. The photo episode explains why, on his flight over the Auca village the next day, Nate had noticed signs of fear among the Indians. When "George" had later appeared, and the Indians' attitude seemed to improve, the men had disregarded their earlier response—with disastrous results.

This new information brought a rather somber note to our beach visit. But before we had time to ponder its full significance, Dawa and Kimo returned to their story, picking up from when the men were killed.

"They heard singing," Rachel said, puzzled.

Walt and I looked at each other. "Who was singing? The five men?"

Rachel asked them my question. Dawa's answer was, "No, their dead bodies were lying on the beach."

"So who was singing?" But Rachel was concentrating too deeply to answer. We could only listen to the excited chatter of Dawa and Kimo and wait for a translation break. Back and forth the dialogue went, as Rachel asked questions and the Indians continued their animated descriptions.

At that point Holly, who had been sitting on a log down the beach and had heard the Indians' voices getting louder, joined us as we waited for the story to conclude. Judging by the facial expressions and the gesturing of Kimo and Dawa, we all knew they were saying something important.

Dawa pointed behind us, then swept her arm over the trees as she spoke. Something had happened over the jungles. It was too critical a time for us to break in with questions. Finally there was a pause. Rachel, herself confounded, then proceeded to tell us a story that we could hardly comprehend, let alone believe.

"After the men were killed, Dawa in the woods and Kimo on the beach heard singing," Rachel said. "As they looked up over the tops of the trees they saw a large group of people. They were all singing, and it looked as if there were a hundred flashlights."

Flashlights?

Rachel explained, "This is the only word for 'bright light' that they know. But they said it was very bright and flashing. Then suddenly it disappeared."

A host of people singing? Flashing lights? What had Kimo and Dawa seen? What did the people look like? Were they talking about angels?

We looked to Rachel for an explanation. But the story surprised her as much as it did us. She had never heard this before. It was so unexpected, so far beyond our own experience.

"They must have made that up," Holly said.

"No, Holly, they wouldn't make that up," Rachel immediately replied. She had heard the Waorani tell stories for many years, and had verified their accuracy again and again.

As we tried to take in what we had just heard, Walt exclaimed, "Through gates of splendor! Do you think the Indians had a glimpse of that splendor?" (He was referring to the title of Elisabeth Elliot's first book, taken from the hymn, "We Rest on Thee." The five men had sung this hymn just before flying out to Palm Beach.)

I recalled the line from the hymn: "When passing through the gates of pearly splendor. . . ." It metaphorically depicts what death is like for a Christian—the grimness giving way to a beautiful scene of glory. Even though I believe that at death, the souls of Christians are transported into God's presence, I don't expect humans to be able to see this take place before their eyes. Had the Indians actually witnessed something that I only knew by faith? Like Holly, I too found it hard not to be skeptical.

Walt and I had no idea whether Kimo and Dawa knew we were struggling to believe their story. But Kimo wanted to say something to Walt. Since Walt was the Bible teacher, he would understand as Kimo tried to relate what they had seen to Scripture. Rachel translated: "When the disciples of Jesus were in the canoe and saw Jesus walking toward them on the water, they were afraid. They thought Jesus was a ghost. We were afraid just like the disciples. We did not know what we had seen. When the disciples knew it was Jesus, they were not afraid. Later, when we heard God's Word, we were no longer afraid."

Kimo's explanation only raised more questions. Standing on the beach, our clothes still soaked from the rain, we tried to sort out what we had heard.

Walt and I wondered if they had invented the story to gain approval. No, that was impossible. It came out far too spontaneously between the two of them. Too much planning would have been required for them to correlate their facts. We all had watched their faces and their elaborate gesturing. There was no question that they had seen *something*.

"Why haven't they told this story to you before?" I asked.

"We haven't talked about the killings for many years," Rachel reminded us. "I couldn't keep on asking questions about how they killed my brother."

We were convinced that Rachel was right: Kimo and Dawa had not made up the story. We guessed that most likely they had been terrified by the vision, and therefore did not talk about it when first questioned about the killings. Perhaps it took years of Bible teaching for them to understand what they had seen. Or possibly, the fuller knowledge of Scripture they now possess led them to embellish their account somewhat. But whatever the explanation, we knew we could not dismiss the story.

Soon the time came for us to leave the beach. My mind reeled with questions and images and memories as I watched Dawa holding her little girl and Kimo making a new bamboo pole for the trip upriver. In a way, they personified the glimpse of eternity that I had sought thirty-three years earlier. After Pete's death, I had been overwhelmed because my known world was gone—dreams dashed, ministry suspended, hope vaporized. Looking desperately for assurance, I remembered writing out a Scripture passage in my journal: "So we do not lose heart. . . . For this slight momentary affliction is preparing for us an eternal weight of glory beyond all comparison, because we look not to the things that are seen, but to the things that are unseen; for the things that are seen are transient, but the things that are unseen are eternal" (2 Corinthians 4:16–18). I had found some comfort in these verses, but also frustration, because I had wanted God to give me a concrete sign—something I could see—to make it easier to trust him in this tragedy. But he didn't.

As we climbed back into the canoe, I wondered if God had chosen instead to display the light of his glory—a glimpse of the unseen—to the fierce and primitive Aucas as they stood on this very beach. Was it possible that he had used the men's fatal mistake as his opportunity to break through to these Aucas, who had been bound by such incredible darkness and evil? Dawa later indicated so. She told Rachel that the vision was what first led her to believe that there was a God. And when Betty and Rachel and Dayuma (who had become a Christian) eventually arrived, Dawa had become the first Christian in the tribe.

I took one last look at Palm Beach as Kimo pushed the canoe out into the river. To me it no longer symbolized death, but rather the beginning of new life for the Waorani people. Over the years the forces of nature had eroded all traces of death on this beach. There is no shrine or grave marker there. The real, lasting memorial to the five men can be found in the strong Christian Waorani leaders, many of whom are the actual killers, their wives, or their relatives. Though Pete, Jim, Ed, Roger, and Nate never had the chance to tell the Waorani about their Lord, their death—and the miraculous aftermath—somehow prepared the first Aucas to embrace the gospel five years later.

But it had all begun on this beach. And two of the people in this canoe had actually been there—Kimo, the vicious killer, and Dawa, the reluctant observer. From that day on, their lives, and the lives of hundreds of Waorani, had begun to follow a new course.

*   *   *

When Holly, Walt, and I returned to the civilized world of the United States, where we seem to depend less on God for our daily needs, and where we tend to be suspicious of the supernatural, we again began to question the vision of the Waoranis. Some months later we talked to Rachel on the phone. She had talked to Dyuwi further about what happened on the beach. (Dyuwi remains a strong Christian and an evangelist among his own people.) He too described a scene of bright lights and a large group of people singing. He even went so far as to mimic the various instruments he had heard. Looking back on the experience, he now concluded that he had seen angels. But whatever (or whoever) it was, there was no question that he had seen something. Rachel does not doubt his word.

As I reflected on the Indians' reports, it occurred to me that in advanced countries such as the United States, many of our own minds are bound in a different way. Overly rationalistic thinking, scientific methods geared to tangible, repeatable results, and a general skepticism toward the supernatural may actually prevent us from believing in visions or other miraculous acts of God. I realized that I needed to allow God to reveal himself to me (and to the Waorani) in any way he pleased, even if it didn't fit my preconceived notions.

Ultimately, whether the Indians' vision was real, or whether it can be verified, is not the issue. What matters most is that we learn to trust God to guide us through the decisions and changes of life, even when there is no bright light from heaven to show us the way. If I have learned anything during my short time with Pete, and in the thirty-three years since he died, it is that I can never know the mind of God. Nor can I evaluate his eternal purposes simply on the basis of what I can see— circumstances, results, even visions.

When Pete broke up with me to become a single missionary, I was devastated. When he was killed, my entire world fell apart. In both cases, I had no idea whatsoever of God's will for my life. All the visible circumstances looked bleak, like those pictured by the prophet Habakkuk: "the fig

tree does not bud . . . no grapes on the vines, . . . olive crop fails
. . . fields produce no food . . . no sheep in the pen and no cattle
in the stalls" (3:17). Amid all this desolation, and without seeing
any results, Habakkuk said, "Yet I will rejoice in the Lord"
(3:18 NIV).

I still find it hard to say these words. Many times I have
felt angry, frustrated, or disappointed with the Lord. I don't
always feel like rejoicing. And I don't always know what my
next step should be. But now I am learning to trust—not in
tangible, temporal things, not in what I think God has done or
is going to do, not even in God's "will" for my life. Instead, I
am learning to trust in God himself. Even when I don't know
the bigger picture, he does.

And what about Pete? He had prayed that God would
make the Ecuadorian jungles into a "proving ground" in which
the world could "watch God act in response to . . . our faith for
his work." He had asked God to show what the gospel could do
in the lives of "immoral, shifty, treacherous people." He never
saw the answer to his prayer. But I did, along with hundreds of
thousands of people around the world. God had indeed
vindicated His name.

In his twenty-seven years of searching for and answering
God's call, Pete Fleming made plenty of mistakes along the
way. (I hasten to add that I also made more than my share.)
There were errors of judgment, errors of timing, errors of
oversight. He appeared to be easily swayed at times by the
forceful personality of Jim Elliot. At times he struggled with
feelings of depression, uselessness, and failure on the mission
field. But even when his mistakes or his struggles bogged him
down, Pete believed that God would ultimately fulfill His
eternal purposes. He believed in the God of the bigger picture.

When Pete and the other men died that Sunday in 1956,
no one thought that God would choose the gory site of their
martyrdom to display his power—his "light"—to the Aucas.

God was working in ways Pete had never anticipated. Only He could have used that opportunity to fulfill His destiny for the Aucas in a way very reminiscent of Isaiah 9:2: "The people who walked in darkness have seen a great light; those who dwelt in a land of deep darkness, on them has light shined." Perhaps this is the most significant "message" one can extract from Pete's life: that God will always accomplish his will—sometimes through our human efforts, and sometimes in spite of them. We may not understand his intent amid the chaos of our lives, but we *can* ultimately trust that he, and only he, is in control.

Notes

Chapter 5

1. Elisabeth Elliot, *Shadow of the Almighty: The Life and Testament of Jim Elliot* (New York: Harper & Row, 1979), 150.

Chapter 7

1. David Dye, "Peter Fleming Was My Friend," *HIS* magazine (May 1956).

2. Elisabeth Elliot, *Shadow of the Almighty: The Life and Testament of Jim Elliot* (New York: Harper & Row, 1979), 48.

3. Ibid., 88.

4. Ibid.

5. Jim Elliot, *The Journals of Jim Elliot,* Elisabeth Elliot, ed. (Old Tappan, N.J.: Revell, 1983), 65.

6. Ibid., 67.

7. Ibid., 153.

8. Ibid., 154–56.

9. Ibid., 156–57.

10. Ibid., 158.

11. Ibid., 342.

12. Ibid., 344.

13. Ibid., 349.

Chapter 8

1. Jim Elliot, *The Journals of Jim Elliot,* Elisabeth Elliot, ed. (Old Tappan, N.J.: Revell, 1983), 279.

2. Ibid., 283.
3. Ibid.
4. David Dye, "Peter Fleming Was My Friend," *HIS* magazine (May 1956).
5. Amy Carmichael, *His Thoughts Said . . . His Father Said* (Fort Washington, Pa.: Christian Literature Crusade, 1958).

Chapter 9

1. Jim Elliot, *The Journals of Jim Elliot,* Elisabeth Elliot, ed. (Old Tappan, N.J.: Revell, 1983), 366.

Chapter 13

1. Jim Elliot, *The Journals of Jim Elliot,* Elisabeth Elliot, ed. (Old Tappan, N.J.: Revell, 1983), 402.
2. Ibid., 404.

Chapter 14

1. Jim Elliot, *The Journals of Jim Elliot,* Elisabeth Elliot, ed. (Old Tappan, N.J.: Revell, 1983), 437.
2. Nate's story is told in Russell T. Hitt, *Jungle Pilot* (New York: Harper & Brothers, 1959).
3. Elliot, *Journals,* 440.
4. Ibid., 449.
5. Ibid., 449–50.

Chapter 15

1. Jim Elliot, *The Journals of Jim Elliot,* Elisabeth Elliot, ed. (Old Tappan, N.J.: Revell, 1983), 463–64.

Chapter 17

1. Elisabeth Elliot, *Through Gates of Splendor* (Wheaton, Ill.: Tyndale, 1981), 130.
2. Ibid., 132.
3. Ibid., 145–46.
4. See Elisabeth Elliot, *Through Gates of Splendor,* and Russell T. Hitt, *Jungle Pilot,* for more details.

Books of Interest

Elisabeth Elliot, *The Savage, My Kinsman* (Ann Arbor, Mich.: Servant, 1981).

————. *Shadow of the Almighty: The Life and Testament of Jim Elliot* (New York: Harper & Row, 1979).

————. *Through Gates of Splendor* (Wheaton, Ill.: Tyndale, 1981).

Jim Elliot, *The Journals of Jim Elliot,* Elisabeth Elliot, ed. (Old Tappan, N.J.: Revell, 1983).

Russell T. Hitt, *Jungle Pilot* (New York: Harper & Brothers, 1959).

Ethel Emily Wallis, *Aucas Downriver* (New York: Harper & Row, 1973).

————. *The Dayuma Story* (New York: Harper & Brothers, 1960).